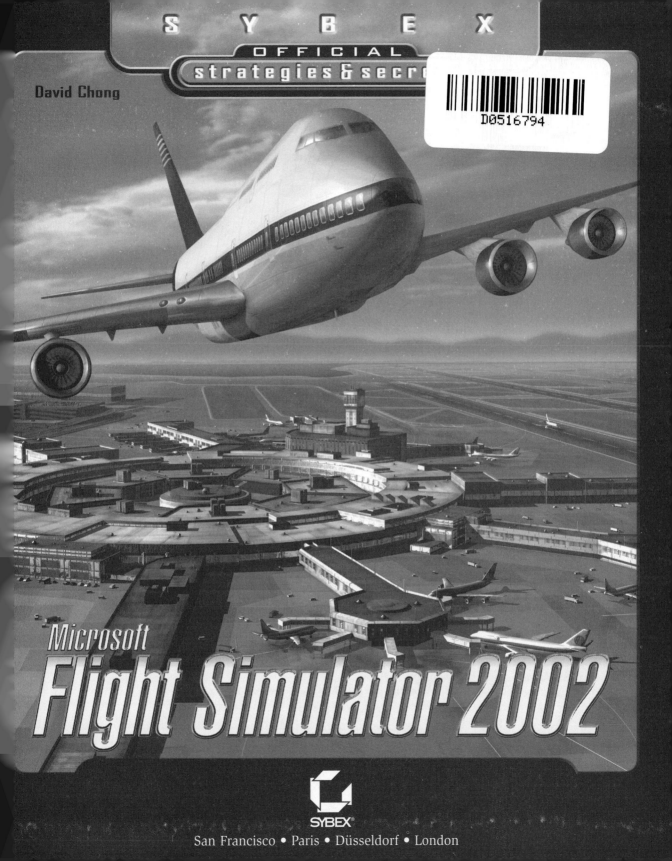

S Y B E X

OFFICIAL
strategies & secr

David Chong

D0516794

Microsoft
Flight Simulator 2002

SYBEX®

San Francisco • Paris • Düsseldorf • London

Associate Publisher	DAN BRODNITZ
Contracts and Licensing Manager	KRISTINE O'CALLAGHAN
Acquisitions and Developmental Editor	WILLEM KNIBBE
Editor	BRETT TODD
Production Editor	MARISA ONG
Technical Editor	ANDY MAHOOD
Proofreader	RICH GANIS
Book Design	OWEN WOLFSON
Book Production	WILLIAM SALIT
Production Assistant	LISA LUSK
Cover Design	RICHARD MILLER, CALYX DESIGN
Poster Design	WILLIAM SALIT

In memory of the innocent people who perished in the tragic airline attacks of September 11, 2001.

Acknowledgments

This strategy guide is the product of a great many wonderful people whose skills and dedication contributed to bringing a top-notch work into your hands. The entire production team deserves particular credit for their long hours and precise work in the final phases of the project. Willem Knibbe, Dan Brodnitz, and Kelly Winquist of the Sybex team have an incredible synergy, which fosters the best work. Brett Todd, copy editor, has worked with me on most of my books and never fails to pick the best path through my original manuscript. Andy Mahood deserves thanks for his technical expertise and late nights. Marisa Ong, William Salit, and Lisa Lusk pulled off a minor miracle with their homestretch efforts.

Microsoft's Bruce Williams and Scott Anderson deserve special kudos for greatly enhancing the book with their thorough, informative, and timely review and explanations. Marty Blaker, Ken Lavering, Jason Waskey, and the rest of the *Flight Simulator 2002* team were characteristically helpful and served as an excellent resource for information and insight into the inner workings of *Flight Simulator 2002*. To all these people, I express my most sincere gratitude for helping create this universal resource for *Flight Sim* pilots.

I must give a very special thank you to my family, Kate and Maggie, in whom my life is centered. There is nothing that helps an author more than the love and support of his best friend and his daughter.

A Letter from the Publisher

Dear Reader,

At Sybex, our goal is to bring you the best game strategy guides money can buy. We hire the best authors in the business, and we bring our love of games to the look and feel of the books. We hope you see all of that reflected in the strategy guide you're holding in your hands right now.

The important question is: How well do YOU think we're doing?

Are we providing you with the kind of in-depth, hardcore gaming content you crave? Is the material presented in a way you find both useful and attractive? Are there other approaches and/or types of information you'd like to see but just aren't getting? Or, are our books so perfect that you're considering nominating them for a Pulitzer this year?

Your comments and suggestions are always valuable. We want to encourage even more feedback from our readers and make it even easier for you to get in touch with us. To that end, we've created an e-mailbox for your feedback. We invite you to send your comments, criticism, praise, and suggestions to gamesfeedback@sybex.com and let us know what you think.

We can't guarantee we'll respond to every message; but we can promise we'll read them all, take them to heart, and then print them out and use the hard copy to make festive hats for everyone in the building.

Most of all, we'll use your feedback to continuously improve the quality of our books. So please, let us hear from you!

Dan Brodnitz
Associate Publisher

Contents

3 Navigation   64

4 Spreading Your Wings   88

OVER THE HORIZON 110

CONQUERING THE SKIES 136

9 Sharing the Sky

224

Introduction

Microsoft Flight Simulator 2002 *is the most realistic and advanced civil aviation simulator available for the home PC today. Its ultra-realistic flight modeling gives you the same experience found in the real skies, and the configuration options allow you to fly anywhere, in any conditions. All of this power can seem somewhat daunting—there's simply so much to know! This guide explores everything that* Flight Simulator 2002 *has to offer, so that the simulation can be fully enjoyed and appreciated.*

The lessons in this guide build upon each other and offer the opportunity to start (or stop) at your level of comfort. A new pilot can start at the beginning of the book and immediately get into the air with the help of this guide and the game's tutorial flights. If you're a veteran aviator, feel free to gloss over the initial sections in Part I: Getting Off the Ground and proceed directly to the advanced concepts found in Part II: Over the Horizon. Conversely, pilots who don't care to take on challenges like creating new aircraft can take full advantage of the flight lessons, procedural information, and activity walkthroughs without ever having to touch the simulation's included gMax editor.

How to Use This Book

The pages that follow serve virtual pilots who are trying on their flight wings for the first time as well as longtime flight simmers. More importantly, people who fall somewhere in-between will be able to find their stride. For example, perhaps you're familiar with aircraft controls and even seat-of-your-pants navigation, but you've never tried using your navigation instruments before. This guide won't bog you down with things you already know. Thanks to clearly labeled topics, you can skip to the information you're interested in and immediately start learning.

Goals of This Guide

This strategy guide is aimed at providing you with two essential resources: a programmed course of instruction and an easy reference guide. The first goal is accomplished by introducing all-new information in steps, so that you can tailor your reading to your particular needs. The second goal is achieved by grouping related information. Of course, all aviation concepts are related in some way, but this logical approach to organization means that you won't have to flip from chapter to chapter to find a tidbit on a given topic.

Organization

Microsoft Flight Simulator 2002: Sybex Official Strategies & Secrets is divided into three Parts, each consisting of several chapters. Part I is a hands-on resource for getting up to speed in general aviation. It is not only for beginners, however, as the checklists found in Chapter 2: Aircraft and Checklists will be used throughout your entire piloting career. The advanced maneuvers and procedures in Chapter 4: Spreading Your Wings are for everyone from budding student pilots to airshow aces.

➤ Chapter 1: Ground School covers start-up information. It's not a rehash of the info found in the online documentation, though; in fact, it provides references to the online manuals that allow you to cut to the chase. It also includes detailed help on tuning your system and the simulation for optimum performance.

➤ Chapter 2: Aircraft and Checklists is a reference tool for every aircraft in the simulator. The online manuals offer excellent background information on each aircraft, and this chapter will help you choose the one that's right for your flight. Each aircraft also has a complete start-up and takeoff checklist, which can be used every time you climb into the plane—whether it's your third time or your three-hundredth!

➤ Chapter 3: Navigation is a complete course of instruction on aerial navigation from the ground up. This chapter benefits from lesson organization that allows an inexperienced pilot to finish the chapter with a complete working knowledge of getting a plane from one point to another.

➤ Chapter 4: Spreading Your Wings takes your piloting skills to the next level. It walks you through several advanced flight procedures, from favorite airshow aerobatics to how to handle in-flight emergencies. *Flight Simulator 2002* offers the ability to customize the chance of failure (including ruling it out entirely), and this chapter will help you set it to suit your taste for aircraft malfunctions.

Part II of this guide offers comprehensive coverage of the advanced concepts in *Flight Simulator 2002*. With the essentials of Part I under your belt, Part II will help you create new flight plans or build completely new adventures.

➤ Chapter 5: Spreading Your Wings deals with creating your own flight plan. It also explains the Flight Planner included in *Flight Simulator 2002*. With it, you can plan flights based upon many different kinds of routing conventions. You'll also learn how to use the information in the online NavLog, helping you make the most of the automated features of *Flight Simulator 2002*.

➤ Chapter 6: Expanding Existing Flights is a look at the options for customizing the Flights menu. You can add new twists to the flights that ship with the simulator, or create entirely new ones. You can share these custom flights with other virtual pilots and even participate in the widespread hobby of virtual airlines.

Part III: Conquering the Skies rounds out the coverage offered by this guide, with detailed analyses of all the new flight activities offered in *Flight Simulator 2002*. These walk-throughs will serve as invaluable tools for those who plan on trying the themed flights. The included tables list all navigation and communication information. No more pausing the game to open up windows—you can keep all the reference information at your fingertips and follow along with the text for each leg of a journey.

➤ Chapter 7: Going Solo features complete walkthroughs of the new civil aviation activities available. Each flight is covered from start-up to shutdown, with comprehensive tables detailing all of the navigational and communication information required on a flight.

➤ Chapter 8: Flying First Class is in the same vein as its predecessor, though it handles the commercial flights new to *Flight Simulator 2002*. As with the civil flights, commercial captains will benefit from the pointers offered on each leg of the trip.

➤ Chapter 9: Sharing the Sky takes *Flight Simulator 2002* to the ultimate level: real-time flight with other virtual pilots in the sky via the various multiplayer modes. This chapter also includes never-before-published information on logging into the expanding world of virtual air traffic control, where a huge network of people is flying realistic flights with the help of live controllers using voice communications.

New Features

Flight Simulator 2002 is the latest in a long line of flight sims from Microsoft. Veteran *Flight Simulator* pilots can use the following list of new features in the latest version to orient themselves with the new material as quickly as possible.

N O T A M
Notice to All Airmen

Please visit www.sybex.com for an online update that features additional strategies for the activities and guidance in using gMax to create, import, and edit scenery, airplanes, and airports.

➤ **Air Traffic Control (ATC):** Realistic ATC communications complete the flight experience in controlled airspace. The new ATC system features realistic procedures, handoffs, and clearances.

➤ **Crowded Skies:** Artificial intelligence generates and controls air traffic in your area, adding to the depth of the simulation. ATC even tracks and handles these robot aircraft.

➤ **Enhanced Virtual Cockpits:** The virtual cockpit view provides *Flight Simulator 2002* pilots with panning views in fully operational cockpits, complete with working indicators and controls.

➤ **Enhanced Visual Effects:** Stunning visual effects that made *Combat Flight Simulator 2* so exciting are now in *Flight Simulator 2002*. You'll see contrails from high-altitude jets, dramatic lighting effects, and puffs of smoke from tires at touchdown.

➤ **Exclusive Content from the Aircraft Owners and Pilots Association (AOPA):** Student pilots and seasoned pros can tap into articles from *AOPA Flight Training* and *AOPA Pilot* magazines.

➤ **Flight Analysis:** A detailed flight recorder logs the vital performance statistics of each flight, allowing you to replay maneuvers in detail for later consideration.

➤ **Flight Instructor Station:** A new two-player option allows one player to act as a flight instructor, inducing failures and controlling the simulation environment to train or challenge another pilot.

➤ **Floatplane Flying:** With the famous Cessna Caravan utility aircraft on floats, you can take off and land from lakes, rivers, and bays all over the world.

➤ **Flying Lessons:** Accomplished flight instructor Rod Machado has engineered a programmed course of instruction that takes you all the way from private pilot to air transport pilot ratings. *Flight Simulator 2002* includes a rating system complete with printable certificates.

> **Graphical Flight Planner:** Plot your route from departure to destination on an interactive map that features automatic or manual routing via great circle or airways.

> **More Scenery, More Locations:** *Flight Simulator 2002* includes coverage of essentially every single published airport and navigational aid in the entire world! Plus, the new scenery system generates localized scenery objects appropriate to the region you're flying over, eliminating the possibility of encountering vast expanses of featureless terrain.

> **New Aircraft:** The Cessna 172, the Cessna 208 Caravan, and the Boeing 747-400 are included for the first time.

> **New Virtual Career Options:** New flight categories allow you to embark upon a virtual flight career in *Flight Simulator 2002*.

> **Powerful Add-on Tools:** A powerful 3D graphic modeling program called gMax is included with the program, allowing you to manipulate the simulator's environment by changing scenery or objects, or even adding your own creations.

> **Terrain Elevations:** The new digital elevation terrain mesh system provides greater detail and realism, while still allowing users to customize the terrain elevation complexity to fit their system capabilities.

Version Differences

This guide covers both the Professional and Standard Editions of *Flight Simulator 2002*. If you are using the Standard Edition, some of the included tools and features mentioned in this guide may not apply. Fear not, though, as both editions are essentially the same in terms of gameplay. The Professional Edition just includes additional aircraft and construction tools for advanced users. All of the fundamental principles, lessons, and concepts apply to both versions, so this guide won't steer you wrong no matter which model you're flying. A summary of the additional features of the Professional Edition are listed below:

> **Additional Aircraft**: The following aircraft are included only in the Professional Edition: Beech Baron 58, Beech King Air 350, Cessna 208B Grand Caravan, and the Mooney Bravo (both versions).

> **gMax Editor**: The Professional Edition includes the powerful gMax 3D graphic editor, which allows you to modify and create objects, including buildings, roads, airports, and even planes.

> **Flight Instructor Station:** A two-player option enables one player to act as a flight instructor and monitor progress, trigger surprise system failures, and control the simulation environment.

Part I
GETTING OFF THE GROUND

This portion of the guide will help every virtual aviator, from the new pilot to the seasoned aviator. The setup tips in Chapter 1 will help you get your system and the simulator into top form, with easy-to-follow instructions for optimizing performance.

Chapter 2 should prove to be an invaluable resource for every pilot, with full start-up and takeoff checklists for every aircraft in the simulator. From there, you'll learn how to actually apply your navigation skills in practice with the navigation instruction in Chapter 3. Finally, pilots of all skill levels will benefit from the advanced maneuvers and procedures detailed in Chapter 4. Whether you're just starting a virtual piloting career or expanding one, you'll find essential information in this section of the guide to help you enjoy Flight Simulator 2002 to its fullest.

CHAPTER 1
Ground School

This chapter contains information that novice pilots and veteran aviators alike need to get into the air with Microsoft Flight Simulator 2002. It begins with tips for optimizing your system's configuration and program settings. We then look at Flight Simulator 2002's in-game settings and discuss peripheral devices that help create an accurate simulation experience.

Configuring the Simulation

Flight Simulator 2002 is one of the most advanced programs on the market today in any field. The simulation pushes the performance of modern desktop systems to the very edge of their capabilities, with demands on everything from raw processing power to displaying graphics to sound mixing. However, it can function equally well on a system that just squeaks by with the minimum system requirements. All that's required is a little bit of tweaking with your system and *Flight Simulator 2002* itself. This section will help you do just that.

Optimizing Your System

There are a few things you can do to make sure that your system is fully capable of running *Flight Simulator 2002* at a reasonable level of performance. Obviously, you could go out and buy the fastest computer with the most advanced features available, but that's not a very realistic

TIP

Be sure to check out the Before You Fly Handbook, included on your Flight Simulator *CDs. It contains a great deal of helpful information for setting up both your system and the simulation.*

solution for most of us. Still, there are some relatively inexpensive upgrades that will make a huge difference in the performance of your entire system, *Flight Simulator 2002* included:

➤ **Buy a 3D graphics card:** While cutting-edge graphics cards run hundreds of dollars, video cards with slightly dated chipsets can be found at affordable prices. For example, you should be able to pick up a card based on the Voodoo 2 or Voodoo 3 chipsets, the ATI Rage chipset, or one of the older NVidia chipsets for under $50. These cards are inexpensive for a reason: they're older and generally feature 8MB or 12MB of Video RAM (VRAM). *Flight Simulator 2002* requires at least 8MB VRAM, and your performance will definitely be better if you spend a bit more and get a card with at least 16MB RAM. Make sure the 3D graphics card you buy is a hardware accelerator, not a software-accelerated 3D card. Many cards call themselves 3D just because they can take advantage of Windows Direct3D software, but there is a great performance difference between 3D software acceleration and 3D hardware acceleration.

➤ **Install more memory:** Memory (also referred to as Random Access Memory, or RAM) is extremely inexpensive these days, and it's one of the easiest components for users to install by themselves. You should upgrade in whatever denomination you can afford, although the price point for 256MB chips is ideal (as of this writing).

Optimizing Windows

The first step in getting the best performance out of any program is to ensure that you're getting top performance out of your Windows operating system. Since Windows is behind every program that runs on your desktop, it makes sense that any program will only run as well as you have Windows configured. Below, you'll find a few techniques for optimizing your Windows configuration.

Most of the following changes will require you to change system settings. For maximum safety, write down the original settings before you implement any changes. This way, you'll be able to easily change them back in case you experience a problem. Also, you will often be asked to reboot your system in order for changes to take effect; do this each time the option is offered, to help ensure stability.

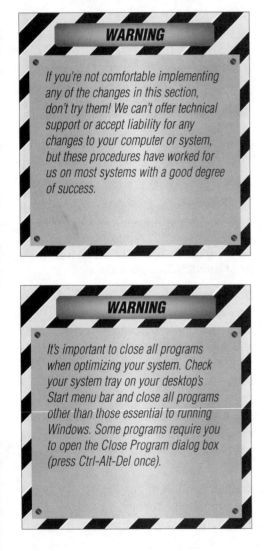

WARNING

If you're not comfortable implementing any of the changes in this section, don't try them! We can't offer technical support or accept liability for any changes to your computer or system, but these procedures have worked for us on most systems with a good degree of success.

WARNING

It's important to close all programs when optimizing your system. Check your system tray on your desktop's Start menu bar and close all programs other than those essential to running Windows. Some programs require you to open the Close Program dialog box (press Ctrl-Alt-Del once).

Disk Defragmentation

Perhaps the easiest system optimization you can perform is to defragment ("defrag") your hard drive(s). As you store and erase information on your computer over time, related materials end up spread all over the place. The defrag process cleans this mess up, putting all related information together. Defragmentation can take over an hour on larger drives, so be sure to schedule the operation when you won't need the computer for a while.

To defragment your drive, follow these steps:

1. Close all programs; e-mail, communications programs, virus scanners, or any other applications that periodically access the hard drive will force the defrag process to start over.

2. Click Start, then Programs, then Accessories, then System Tools, and then Disk Defragmenter.

3. At the Select Drive prompt, you should be defaulted to the C: physical drive. If so, click OK; otherwise, use the drop-down menu to select the C: physical drive before clicking OK.

Virtual Memory Settings

By default, Windows 95 and 98 use a system called virtual memory to let your computer act as if it has more physical RAM than it actually does. Virtual memory has many advantages, but it does come with some drawbacks as well. First, information stored on your hard drives is retrieved much more slowly than information stored in physical memory. Second, Windows dynamically controls the size of your virtual memory cache, meaning that it constantly monitors your need and changes its size as necessary. This is a burden on your processor and does cause some performance degradation.

To fix this in Windows 95 and 98 (for later versions of Windows, please consult the operating system's Help), do the following:

1. Open System Properties in Control Panel by selecting Start, then Settings, and then Control Panel.

2. Select the Performance tab. Make a note of the amount of memory you have installed, as shown at the top of the dialog box.

3. Click the Virtual Memory button on the bottom of the window. On the next screen, select "Let me specify my own virtual memory settings" by clicking the appropriate radio button.

4. In the boxes below, select your fastest hard drive from the pull-down menu. Some people have installed newer hard drives as a drive D: or higher; if you have a newer and faster drive installed, select it instead of your C: drive.

5. You want 640MB of memory in your system, as a total of your physical RAM and your virtual memory. Remembering the amount of memory installed in your system from the display above, enter an amount that will add up to 640MB in the Minimum and Maximum fields. So if your system has 256MB of physical RAM, type **384** into both fields to give you a total of 640MB. By setting the minimum and maximum to the same size, your computer won't waste processor cycles managing it.

Optimizing the Simulation Settings

Flight Simulator 2002 is fully customizable, allowing you to tailor the simulation's processing demands to your computer's specific configuration. You can set the simulator to display sparse terrain with no frills, full-screen 3D with accelerated high-resolution graphics and computer-controlled planes filling the sky, or anything in between. This wide range of options means that a wide range of computers can successfully run the simulation. You can access all of the simulator's options through the Settings screen, shown in Figure 1.1.

All settings in a demanding program like *Flight Simulator* should be seen as compromises. Unless you have the latest and greatest hardware across the board (processor, motherboard, RAM, graphics card, etc.), you probably won't be able to run the simulation with all

Figure 1.1 The Settings screen offers powerful configuration options.

of the settings maxed out. However, that's not really necessary for an excellent sim experience. All you have to do is learn to balance performance with features.

The simulation can push your computer to the limit. Go beyond the limit, and *Flight Simulator 2002* will run too slowly to be enjoyed. Every feature you turn on takes up some

Frame Rates

One universal requirement in Flight Simulator 2002 *is frame rate. This term is a measure of how many picture frames per second (FPS) are displayed on your screen. A frame rate of about 11 FPS is the absolute minimum acceptable, and most people prefer a minimum frame rate of 16 FPS or more. Anything less results in some strange situations because of display lag.*

At very low frame rates, the difference between what the simulation is doing and what you actually see on the screen can be significant. Eventually, you will see things too late to react to them. For example, you won't be able to tell when to center your controls when banking, because you will see the plane jerking around in response to input sent earlier.

To see your current frame rate, press "Shift-Z" twice. The first time you press it, you'll see your plane's coordinates displayed. The second will bring up the frame rate display, which shows both the FPS and your current G-loads (which are described in Chapter 4: Spreading Your Wings). Use this display liberally when tweaking your simulator settings. It provides useful feedback on the effects that your selections are having on overall simulation performance. By changing one thing at a time and then looking at the frame rate, you'll see which settings have the most effect on your computer system and you can plan further tweaks accordingly.

of your PC's resources, so the trick is to figure out which features are important to you and which you can live without. Your ultimate goal should be to tailor the settings to give you performance within the bounds of your computer's capabilities, while still delivering all the features that you want.

The central compromise in all settings is speed versus quality and quantity. On one side of the equation are smooth motion, crisp control response, seamless instrument displays, and generally fast performance. Weighing against this is the natural desire for an environment that looks and feels as real as possible, with highly detailed graphics, dense terrain features near the ground, air traffic and dynamic scenery, and other features that simply make everything look better.

Display Settings

Your first stop should be the Display Settings menu. This controls all aspects of the look of the simulator, which has the greatest overall impact on performance. The first tab is the Scenery menu. This section controls all of the specific scenery settings. Before fiddling with the individual settings, try the drop-down Global Scenery Settings menu. If your system is near the minimum requirements, try choosing Low here. Medium befits the recommended system, and High is best for systems that exceed the recommended requirements. Choose the Extremely High setting only if your computer is truly cutting-edge.

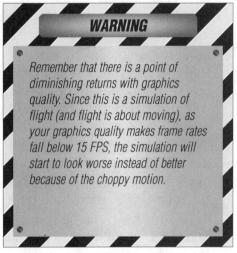

WARNING

Remember that there is a point of diminishing returns with graphics quality. Since this is a simulation of flight (and flight is about moving), as your graphics quality makes frame rates fall below 15 FPS, the simulation will start to look worse instead of better because of the choppy motion.

Note that each setting's impact on performance is also greatly dependent upon where you fly. Flying over Denver, the water effects setting will have little effect on performance, but the terrain mesh will have a huge impact because of the mountainous topography. Conversely, spend most of your time crossing the Atlantic at night and in fog, and there will be no difference in performance even with terrain texture qualities maxed out, since no terrain textures can be displayed!

Below is a general look at each Scenery setting. As noted above, your mileage may vary depending upon the conditions and locations in which you fly.

➤ **Scenery Texture Quality:** Scenery Texture Quality controls the appearance of the surfaces of the scenery in the simulation. Everything you see in *Flight Simulator 2002* is made up of polygons, which have "painted" surfaces used to suggest details. For example, a building might look like it has windows, doors, trim, and so on, when it is really just a flat wall with those details painted on it. The higher the texture quality, the better those details will look.

➤ **Terrain Mesh Complexity:** This setting governs the distance between each elevation point on the ground, which determines the size of the polygons that make up ground features. More polygons mean more detailed terrain. Polygon count is also a sure-fire way to slow down performance, so be careful with this one.

➤ **Terrain Texture Size:** This controls the distance at which you see complex scenery. The higher this setting, the greater the distance at which you'll see detailed, high-resolution terrain. Obviously, this will take its toll on performance, so use it sparingly.

➤ **Autogen Density:** New for *Flight Simulator 2002*, the Autogen Density setting creates trees, buildings, and other appropriate objects in places where specific ground objects haven't already been placed. This helps the world look more realistic and populated. The denser the setting, the more often you'll encounter these objects. Autogen causes a moderate performance hit.

➤ **Scenery Complexity:** All of the scenery objects in the simulation are controlled here. Higher settings mean more buildings, trees, roads, towers, and everything else that sits on the ground. This can cause a significant hit on frame rates, but it's also one of the frills that makes flying the simulator enjoyable if you're using visual flight rules or sightseeing. Conversely, if you mostly fly at high altitude or in inclement weather, you won't notice much difference except when landing and taking off.

➤ **Scenery Effects:** This setting should be kept fairly high, as most special effects appear rarely and the overall performance hit is negligible. If you want to see jet contrails and the Extra 300S's smoke trails but your system is bogging down, this is the setting to adjust.

➤ **Maximum Visibility:** Absolute maximum visibility range before things are fogged out at the horizon is handled here. The higher you set it, the farther you'll see into the distance. This setting has the greatest effect on slower computers. If it's important to see your immediate surroundings, trade distance for local quality.

➤ **Water Effects:** This turns on wave action along coastlines. If you fly close enough to see them, you'll take a performance hit, so beware—you don't want to be pushing 12 FPS and then wander into a beach area, as your frame rate would drop and you might be unable to control the plane.

➤ **Dynamic Scenery:** This setting adjusts how much dynamic scenery, including air traffic, appears. The more dynamic scenery you select, the more your PC's resources will be taxed.

Similar setting options are included for the aircraft models in the game. If you like using the chase plane or tower views, use higher settings on the Exterior Texture Size and Global Aircraft Quality options. And if you use the virtual cockpit for anything other than occasional sightseeing, you'll want to use a higher quality there. Checkboxes for the individual effects (shown in Figure 1.2) do have an effect on performance—turning off shadows is one way to

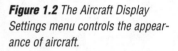

Figure 1.2 *The Aircraft Display Settings menu controls the appearance of aircraft.*

gain an extra frame or two immediately. Reflections look beautiful, but they also cost quite a bit of processor time.

The last tab in the Display Settings menu is called Hardware. The resolution you use will have one of the most significant effects on your frame rates. A minimum machine should use 640x480, and you can go up from there depending on your system capabilities. Note that 3D visuals work only when flying the simulation in full-screen mode, so always use this setting if you're pushing your performance with a true 3D card. Hardware Rendering Options improve the overall texture quality, but they do have a noticeable effect on performance.

Gear Up!

Much of the enjoyment when flying a simulator comes from getting as close as you can to the real thing. There are a few things that you can do to help re-create some of the authentic flying experience, and this section examines those methods.

The Flight Controller

One of the most significant ways to enhance your experience with *Flight Simulator 2002* is to use full-featured controllers. While any two-button joystick performs the absolute minimum pitch and roll functions, having a controller similar to the ones in real aircraft helps you feel like you're really in a plane. Since you don't have any other physical sensations of flight (no inertial forces, no wind in your hair, no smells of engine oil), the controls in your hand are really your only physical tie to flying and, therefore, are extremely important.

Joysticks

A joystick is the most practical way to control your simulator. It can be used for *Flight Simulator 2002* and as your primary controller for any other software title that makes use of a standard joystick. This makes it an investment in fun that can cover multiple games, which certainly makes the most sense for those concerned with the bottom line.

WARNING

Not all hat switches are the same. Some offer only four-way viewing, which restricts your control to the four cardinal directions. This is almost useless for taxiing and navigation, when you need your front quarters. Look for a stick that has an eight-way hat switch.

At their most basic, joysticks are simple two-axis affairs with two or four buttons. It might be a good idea to spend a few extra dollars to purchase a quality stick. If you crank away on your joystick while powering through a high-G maneuver, you can exert serious forces on its components. A broken stick that you have to replace is more expensive than the durable one you bought only once.

When selecting a stick, pay special attention to the gimbals, mechanical links that allow the stick to pivot. These are usually the first things to give way in a stick, so look for strong construction. Microsoft has a complete line of versatile, affordable joysticks in the SideWinder family. Both the Precision 2 and Force Feedback 2 models offer eight-way hat switches and rudder controls. For more information, check out `http://www.microsoft.com/hardware/sidewinder/sidewinder.asp`.

Saitek makes a base-model joystick line with an innovative spring system that will probably outlast your PC. They are a good choice for pilots who aren't looking to spend a lot on a controller, since they still offer features such as multiple buttons and a separate throttle like their more expensive cousins (see Figure 1.3).

For the ultimate joystick suite, try one with a separate throttle (sometimes called a HOTAS, which is short for Hands On Throttle And Stick). This type of stick is more expensive than a basic model, but you might find the features make it worth the extra cost. These sticks are readily available in most computer stores, which puts them within reach of the average armchair pilot. Thrustmaster produces a popular stick and throttle combo called the Top Gun Afterburner, shown in Figure 1.4. The Afterburner includes eight buttons, an eight-way hat switch to change views, a full-throttle handle, and a selectable rudder that allows you to control the rudder by either twisting the stick or by using a fingertip rocker switch on the far side of the throttle handle. Stick twisting is a common feature these days, but you can get more precise control from the throttle rocker, making this controller very attractive

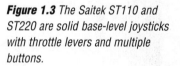

Figure 1.3 The Saitek ST110 and ST220 are solid base-level joysticks with throttle levers and multiple buttons.

Figure 1.4 The Thrustmaster Top Gun Afterburner is an excellent full-featured joystick and throttle suite.

for the *Flight Simulator* pilot. Also, the joystick and throttle can be screwed together into a single unit for use on cramped desks, or even in your lap.

Flight yokes and rudder pedals are the closest thing you can get to the controls found in most civil aircraft, but they're hard to find in retail outlets. If you're willing to order through the mail, you can find flight yoke systems with various feature sets available for purchase direct from the manufacturers. You can also get rudder pedal systems. Be sure that they are compatible with the flight yoke you select, though, as even some systems made by the same manufacturers are not compatible with all of their products. This sometimes makes the business of selecting a yoke and pedal system a complicated process. However, you can find some great hints and tips online by surfing to `http://www.flightsim.com` for information and reviews of some of the systems available. The manufacturers' Web sites also include useful feature information.

Sound

Your sound system should not be underestimated when considering flight hardware. *Flight Simulator 2002* faithfully reproduces the sounds of being in flight, and your system should take full advantage of them with a proper sound card and speaker system. Faint, scratchy, or tinny sounds will constantly remind you that you're in your home or office sitting at a keyboard.

The most common type of sound card is a 16-bit model. You can also go to the other extreme with 128-bit cards that have radio tuners, mixing boards, and a host of other stuff that you might not need. The best way to go is with a straightforward card made especially for gaming. There are several on the market today that are available for under $60.

Speakers are probably even more important than your sound card. Almost all sound cards can at least do a passable job at sound processing, but unamplified, low-quality speakers probably won't do a very good job of properly imaging the throaty roar of a 747's engines. Your local electronics superstore often has specials on amplified speakers that provide a much more exciting aural atmosphere for around $25. Spend a little more and you can get a subwoofer, which is a box that specializes in producing deep bass sounds—perfect for a little kick in the pants when something exciting happens!

Your First Flight

With your system optimized, the simulator configured, and your peripherals in place, you're ready to fly! The quick reference card included with *Flight Simulator 2002* includes step-by-step instructions on getting in the air for free flight. Feel free to ignore air traffic control, airspace restrictions, and even destination concerns—just get up there and fly! If you select a populated area such as southern California or the U.S. Eastern seaboard, you'll find a place to land simply by flying in any direction (except maybe out to sea) for a long enough time.

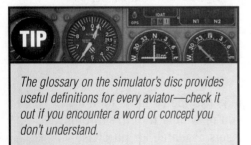

The glossary on the simulator's disc provides useful definitions for every aviator—check it out if you encounter a word or concept you don't understand.

For information on creating a specific flight plan, turn to Chapter 6. Therein you'll find a detailed examination of the considerations that shape a formal flight plan, and you'll learn how to create any flight plan you want. Chapters 7 and 8 provide you with walkthroughs of the simulator's new flight activities, which are themed flights, complete with background situations and fully programmed flight plans. Choose any of them, and flip to the appropriate walkthrough for a full-fledged flight experience!

CHAPTER 2
Aircraft and Checklists

You can find comprehensive information about every aircraft in Flight Simulator 2002 in the Aircraft Handbook section of the on-disc manual. The Aircraft Handbook includes flight notes, details about each aircraft, and a brief history of each aircraft. This chapter expands upon the information presented there by giving you the specific v-speeds for each aircraft and detailed, step-by-step takeoff checklists for getting into the air.

Beechcraft

From the single engine, V-tailed Bonanza to the luxurious and powerful Beechjet, Beechcraft remains a household name in the aviation industry. *Flight Simulator 2002 Professional Edition* includes two Beechcraft aircraft, the Baron 58 piston twin and the King Air 350, a pressurized, twin-engine turboprop. Both aircraft highlight Beechcraft's strong presence in the private and light commercial and provide excellent endurance, making them a natural choice for longer cross-country flights, group charters, or executive shuttle services.

N O T A M
Notice to All Airmen

Beechcraft planes are only included in the Professional Edition of *Flight Simulator 2002*, so you won't see them listed if you're flying the Standard Edition.

Beech Baron 58

The Beech Baron 58's luxurious appointments and work-horse performance place it at the top of the light-twin market. With a range of over 1,500 nautical miles (NM) and its ability to carry a heavy load, the Baron makes an excellent choice for a private pilot looking to fly a family or group of up to five passengers to virtually any destination.

N O T A M
Notice to All Airmen

All v-speeds in this chapter assume flaps up (except for the Boeing jets, where flap settings are noted), 5,000' pressure altitude, and standard temperature.

Figure 2.1 *Beech Baron 58*

Performance Data

V-SPEED	INDICATED AIRSPEED IN KNOTS
VA – Maneuvering Speed	156 KIAS
VFE – Maximum Flaps Extended Speed	152 KIAS (approach, flaps 15)
	122 KIAS (full down, flaps 30)
VLE – Maximum Landing Gear Extension Speed	152 KIAS
VLO – Maximum Gear Operating Speed	152 KIAS
VREF – Landing Approach Speed (5,400 lbs.)	95 KIAS (full down, flaps 30)
VNO – Maximum Structural Cruising Speed	195 KIAS
Turbulent Air Penetration Speed	156 KIAS
VNE – Never Exceed Speed	223 KIAS
VS – Stalling Speed (maximum weight)	84 KIAS
VSO – Stalling Speed in the Landing Configuration (maximum weight)	75 KIAS
VX – Two-Engine Best Angle-of-Climb Speed	92 KIAS
VY – Two-Engine Best Rate-of-Climb Speed	105 KIAS
VXSE – One-Engine Inoperative Best Angle-of-Climb Speed	100 KIAS
VYSE – One-Engine Inoperative Best Rate-of-Climb Speed	101 KIAS
Minimum Icing Conditions Speed	130 KIAS
VMCA – Air Minimum Control Speed (single engine)	84 KIAS
Maximum Glide Range Speed	115 KIAS

TAKEOFF CHECKLIST
PLANE MODEL NAME (ALL VARIANTS)

Form Approved No. FS2002-0001

MS Department of Simulation
Sybex Aviation Administration

2. AIRCRAFT TAIL NUMBER

INSTRUCTIONS: *Personally complete all inspections prior to takeoff*

1. NAME *(Last, first, middle)*

3. DATE *(Month/Day/Year)*
/   /

4. FLIGHT INFORMATION

Point of Departure

Destination

INITIAL CHECKS

❏ Parking Brake – SET

❏ All Avionics – OFF

❏ Landing Gear Handle – DOWN

❏ Cowl Flaps – OPEN

❏ Fuel Selectors – ON

❏ All Switches and Equipment Controls – CHECK

❏ Battery and Alternator Switches – ON

❏ Fuel Quantity Indicators – CHECK QUANTITY

LEFT ENGINE START-UP

❏ Select Left Engine ("E," then "1" for Left engine)

❏ Mixture Control – FULL RICH (Ctrl-Shift-F3)

❏ Propeller Control – HIGH RPM (Ctrl-F3)

❏ Throttle – FULL OPEN

❏ Fuel Boost Pump Switch – HI UNTIL FUEL FLOW PEAKS, THEN OFF

❏ Throttle – CLOSE; THEN OPEN APPROX. 1/2 INCH

❏ Magneto/Starter Switch – START position, release to BOTH position when engine starts

❏ Throttle – 900 to 1000 RPM AFTER START

❏ Oil Pressure – 10 PSI WITHIN 30 SECONDS

❏ Alternator Switch – ON

❏ Loadmeters and Voltmeter – CHECK FOR BATTERY CHARGE

❏ Red *START* Annunciator Light – CHECK (should be illuminated during start and extinguished after start)

❏ REPEAT PROCEDURE FOR RIGHT ENGINE ("E," then "2")

AFTER STARTING

❏ Avionics – ON, AS REQUIRED

❏ Exterior Lights – AS REQUIRED

❏ Brakes – RELEASE AND CHECK

BEFORE TAXI (RUNUP)

❏ Parking Brake – SET

❏ Fuel Boost Pumps – OFF (LOW if temp above 32 degrees C)

❏ All Instruments – CHECK

❏ Fuel Indicators – CHECK QUANTITY INDICATED

❏ Mixture – ADJUST AS REQUIRED BY FIELD ELEVATION WHEN SETTING FULL POWER FOR TAKEOFF

❏ Fuel Selectors – CHECK ON

❏ Red *START* Annunciator Light – CHECK

❏ Master Switch – ON

❏ Throttles – 2200 RPM

❏ Propellers – EXERCISE (establish 200–300 RPM drop, then return to high RPM)

❏ Throttles – 1700 RPM

❏ Magnetos – CHECK (click each to L, R, L, Both, look for <150 RPM drop on each, <50 RPM drop between)

❏ Throttles – 1500 RPM

❏ Propellers – FEATHERING CHECK (no more than 300 RPM drop)

❏ Throttles – IDLE (note RPM or engine stall)

❏ Throttles – 900 to 1000 RPM

❏ Trim – AS REQUIRED FOR TAKEOFF

❏ Flaps – CHECK AND SET FOR TAKEOFF (50% or as required by field)

❏ Flight Controls – CHECK PROPER DIRECTION AND FREEDOM OF MOVEMENT

❏ Ice Protection Systems – AS REQUIRED

❏ Parking Brake – OFF

TAKEOFF
❏ Minimum Takeoff Oil Temperature – 24 degrees C
❏ Throttles – FULL
❏ Propellers – MAX RPM
❏ Mixture – FULL RICH
❏ Airspeed – ROTATE AT Vr (approx. 100 knots)
❏ Landing Gear – RETRACT AFTER TAKEOFF

Date	Signature

Beech King Air 350

The Beech King Air reigns supreme as the most widely used cabin-class turboprop in the world, at times representing 90% of such aircraft worldwide. As with all of Beech's offerings, the aircraft is beautiful throughout, boasting double-club seats, a state-of-the-art entertainment system, and a galley to support as many as 11 passengers plus crew on flights of up to 1,800 miles! The luxury, speed, and capacity of this aircraft make it the natural choice for interregional VIP shuttle services, executive transportation, and first-class charters.

Figure 2.2 *Beech King Air 350*

Performance Data

V-SPEED	INDICATED AIRSPEED IN KNOTS
V1 – Takeoff Decision Speed	108 KIAS (15,000 lbs.)
	104 KIAS (<10,500 lbs.)
VR – Rotation Speed	111 KIAS (15,000 lbs.)
	104 KIAS (<10,500 lbs.)
VA – Maneuvering Speed	184 KIAS (.58 Mach)
V2 – Takeoff Safety Speed	117 KIAS (15,000 lbs.)
	111 KIAS (<10,500 lbs.)
VNE – Never Exceed Speed	263 KIAS
VFE – Maximum Flaps Extended Speed	202 KIAS (approach)
	158 KIAS (fully down)
VLE – Maximum Landing Gear Extension Speed	184 KIAS
VLO – Maximum Gear Operating Speed	184 KIAS (extension)
	166 KIAS (retraction)
Turbulent Air Penetration Speed	170 KIAS
VX – Two-Engine Best Angle-of-Climb Speed	125 KIAS
VY – Two-Engine Best Rate-of-Climb Speed	140 KIAS
VMC – Air Minimum Control Speed	94 KIAS (flaps up)
	93 KIAS (flaps approach)
Maximum Glide Range Speed	135 KIAS
VREF – Landing Approach Speed	109 KIAS (15,000 lbs.)
	105 KIAS (14,000 lbs.)
	102 KIAS (13,000 lbs.)
	100 KIAS (12,000 lbs.)
	100 KIAS (11,000 lbs.)
	100 KIAS (10,000 lbs.)

TAKEOFF CHECKLIST
PLANE MODEL NAME (ALL VARIANTS)

Form Approved No. FS2002-0002

MS Department of Simulation
Sybex Aviation Administration

2. AIRCRAFT TAIL NUMBER

INSTRUCTIONS: *Personally complete all inspections prior to takeoff*

1. NAME *(Last, first, middle)*

3. DATE *(Month/Day/Year)*
/   /

4. FLIGHT INFORMATION

Point of Departure	Destination

INITIAL CHECKS

❏ Parking Brake – SET

❏ Landing Gear Control – DOWN

❏ Power Levers – IDLE

❏ Propeller Controls – FULL FORWARD (Ctrl-F3)

❏ Condition Levers – FUEL CUTOFF (Ctrl-Shift-F2)

❏ Fuel Quantity Indicators – CHECK QUANTITY

❏ Anti-Ice – ON

❏ Beacon – ON

❏ Anti-Ice Annunciators – CHECK ILLUMINATED (Shift-5)

ENGINE START-UP

❏ Battery Switch – ON

❏ Beacon – CHECK ON

❏ Propeller Area – CHECK CLEAR

❏ Fuel Flow – ON (Ctrl-Shift-F4)

❏ Right Ignition and Engine Start Switch – ON (hold until engine starts)

❏ Right Condition Lever – LOW IDLE (12% MINIMUM)

❏ Right ITT and N1 Turbine RPM – MONITOR

❏ *R FUEL PRESS LOW* Annunciator – EXTINGUISHED (Shift-6)

❏ *R OIL PRESS LOW* Annunciator – EXTINGUISHED

❏ Right Oil Pressure – CHECK

❏ Right Condition Lever – HIGH IDLE

❏ Right Generator – ON

❏ Left Ignition and Engine Start Switch – ON (hold until engine starts)

❏ Left Condition Lever – LOW IDLE (12% MINIMUM)

❏ Left ITT and N1 Turbine RPM – MONITOR

❏ *L FUEL PRESS LOW* Annunciator – EXTINGUISHED (Shift-6)

❏ *L OIL PRESS LOW* Annunciator – EXTINGUISHED

❏ Left Oil Pressure – CHECK

❏ Left Condition Lever – HIGH IDLE

❏ Left Generator – ON

❏ Avionics Master Switch – ON

BEFORE TAXI (RUNUP)

❏ Avionics – CHECK

❏ Autopilot – CHECK

❏ Electronic Pitch Trim Control – CHECK

❏ Trim Tabs – SET

❏ Primary Governors – EXERCISE AT 1500 RPM

❏ Autofeather – ARM

❏ Manual Propeller Feathering – CHECK

❏ Anti-Ice – AS REQUIRED

❏ Fuel Quantity, Flight, and Engine Instruments – CHECK

BEFORE TAKEOFF (FINAL CHECK)

❏ Annunciator Lights – EXTINGUISHED OR CONSIDERED

❏ Transponder – ON ALT

❏ Lights – AS REQUIRED

❏ Anti-Ice – AS REQUIRED

❏ Takeoff Speeds (V1, Vr, and V2) – CONFIRM

❏ Flaps – AS REQUIRED

TAKEOFF

❏ Brakes – HOLD

❏ Power Levers – 100% N1 TURBINE RPM

❏ Brakes – RELEASE

❏ Airspeed – ROTATE AT Vr (approx. 110 knots)

❏ Attitude – APPROX 10 DEGREES PITCH UP	
❏ Airspeed – MAINTAIN V2 UNTIL CLEAR OF OBSTACLES	
❏ Flaps – UP (blue line, 125 KIAS minimum)	
❏ Landing Gear – RETRACT AFTER TAKEOFF	
Date	**Signature**

Bell

If you're going to have only one helicopter in your simulator, it might as well be an incarnation of the ubiquitous JetRanger series. The highly regarded Bell 206B JetRanger III is employed around the world in military service, as a corporate transport, rescue service/medevac vehicle, police unit, and in television reporting.

The Bell 206B JetRanger III

Naturally, piloting a helicopter is a completely different experience from fixed-wing aircraft operation. However, there's still an engine, the vehicle still goes up in the air, and there are still procedures you can use to get off the ground in perfect form. The online manuals included on the simulator's CDs contain help with flying a helicopter. There is also a tutorial within the simulation that will teach you the elements of rotary flight.

Figure 2.3 *Bell 206B JetRanger III*

There's little question about when a helicopter fits your needs over a fixed-wing aircraft. Loitering, hovering, landing on rooftops or unprepared surfaces, and a host of other activities are best handled in a chopper. Helicopters can even be your best choice for point-to-point travel when considering *all* travel time—for example, if you're going from one suburban office to another within a couple hundred miles, the time you save going to and from airports can be significant.

Performance Data

V-SPEED	INDICATED AIRSPEED IN KNOTS
Autorotation Maximum Speed	100 KIAS
Autorotation Minimum Descent Speed	52 KIAS
Autorotation Maximum Glide Speed	69 KIAS
Maximum Rate of Climb	52 KIAS (N2 engine RPM 100%)
VNE – Never Exceed Speed	130 KIAS (<3,000 lbs., sea level 3,000' density altitude, decrease 3.5 KIAS per 1,000' above 3,000')
	122 KIAS (>3,000 lbs., sea level 3,000' density altitude, decrease 7.0 KIAS per 1,000' above 3,000')

TAKEOFF CHECKLIST
PLANE MODEL NAME (ALL VARIANTS)

Form Approved No. FS2002-0003

MS Department of Simulation

Sybex Aviation Administration

2. AIRCRAFT TAIL NUMBER

INSTRUCTIONS: *Personally complete all inspections prior to takeoff*

1. NAME *(Last, first, middle)*

3. DATE *(Month/Day/Year)*
/   /

4. FLIGHT INFORMATION

Point of Departure

Destination

BEFORE TAKEOFF

❏ Fuel Quantity Indicators – CHECK QUANTITY

❏ Engine and Transmission Instruments – CHECK WITHIN LIMITS

❏ Lights – AS REQUIRED

❏ Radios and Avionics – SET

❏ Throttle – FULL OPEN

❏ Power and Flight Instruments – SET AND CHECK

❏ Power Turbine (N2) – SET FOR 100% in flat pitch

TAKEOFF

❏ Collective Pitch – INCREASE TO HOVER

❏ Engine Instruments – CHECK

❏ Directional Control – AS REQUIRED

❏ Cyclic Control – AS REQUIRED

❏ Collective – AS REQUIRED

Date

Signature

Boeing

Ah, the big boys! Boeing is the manufacturer of all the "heavies" you'll fly in the retail version of *Flight Simulator 2002* (although you can find offerings from Airbus, McDonnell Douglas, and many others online). These aircraft are commercial movers of hundreds of passengers and thousands of pounds of cargo to worldwide destinations, and they require a skill set all their own to pilot effectively.

Boeing 737-400

The 737 series comprises the most popular jetliners in the world today. With a solid, versatile design, the 737 is easy to use, easy to fly, and easy to maintain. Furthermore, its stout airframe is very adaptable, allowing operators to customize the aircraft to meet specific regional or operational needs. The twin-engine design is predictable and stable, making the 737 the best choice for a budding commercial pilot to use for the transition from private light aircraft to airliners.

Figure 2.4 *Boeing 737-400*

Performance Data

V-SPEED	INDICATED AIRSPEED IN KNOTS
V1 – Takeoff Decision Speed	152 KIAS (143,000 lbs.)
	145 KIAS (132,000 lbs.)
VR – Rotation Speed	157 KIAS (143,000 lbs.)
	149 KIAS (132,000 lbs.)
V2 – Takeoff Safety Speed	161 KIAS (143,000 lbs.)
	155 KIAS (132,000 lbs.)

V-SPEED	INDICATED AIRSPEED IN KNOTS	
Maximum Flap (Placard) Speeds	Flaps	KIAS
	1	230
	2	230
	5	225
	10	210
	15	195
	25	190
	30	185
	40	158
VLE – Maximum Landing Gear Extension Speed	270 KIAS (.82 Mach)	
VLO – Maximum Gear Operating Speed	235 KIAS	
Turbulent Air Penetration Speed	280 KIAS/ (.73 Mach)	
Maximum Glide Range Speed	147 KIAS (136,400 lbs.)	
	144 KIAS (132,000 lbs.)	
VMO – Maximum Operating Speed (airspeed)	340 KIAS (.82 Mach)	

TAKEOFF CHECKLIST **PLANE MODEL NAME (ALL VARIANTS)**	Form Approved No. FS2002-0004
MS Department of Simulation Sybex Aviation Administration	**2. AIRCRAFT TAIL NUMBER**
INSTRUCTIONS: *Personally complete all inspections prior to takeoff*	
1. NAME *(Last, first, middle)*	**3. DATE** *(Month/Day/Year)* / /

4. FLIGHT INFORMATION

Point of Departure	Destination

INITIAL CHECKS

❏ Parking Brake – SET

ENGINE START-UP

❏ Ground Crew Assisted Start-Up – SIGNAL (Ctrl-E)

AFTER START

❏ Engine Start Switches – CHECK GEN

❏ Pitot Heat – ON

❏ De-Ice – AS REQUIRED

❏ Engine Start Levers – CHECK IDLE

❏ Lights – AS REQUIRED

❏ Autopilot – SET and OFF

❏ Instruments – CHECK

❏ Autobrake Switch – RTO

❏ Avionics Switch – ON

❏ Avionics – SET

❏ Request Pushback – SIGNAL (Shift-P)

TAXI

❏ Brakes – RELEASE

❏ Thrust Levers – INCREASE SLIGHTLY TO ROLL

❏ Thrust Levers – IDLE FOR TAXI

❏ Flight Controls – CHECK

❏ Flaps – SET FOR TAKEOFF (5)

❏ Brakes – SET

CLEARED FOR TAKEOFF

❏ Engine Start Switches – GEN

❏ Flight Director – ON

❏ Autothrottle – ARM (if using TO/GA mode for takeoff)

❏ Transponder – ON

❏ Lights – AS REQUIRED

TAKEOFF

❏ Brakes – RELEASE

❏ Thrust Levers – ADVANCE SMOOTHLY TO 40% N1

❏ Thrust Levers – ADVANCE SMOOTHLY TO 100% N1 -OR- TO/GA Mode – ENGAGE

❏ Engine Instruments – MONITOR

❏ Airspeed 80 KIAS – CALL OUT *80 KNOTS.*

❏ Thrust Levers – VERIFY PROPER SETTING
❏ Airspeed V1 – CALL OUT *V1*
❏ Airspeed VR – CALL OUT *ROTATE*, ROTATE TO APPROX. 10 DEGREES PITCH UP
❏ Airspeed V2 – CALL OUT *V2*
❏ Landing Gear – RETRACT AFTER TAKEOFF
❏ Airspeed – MAINTAIN V2+20 KIAS
❏ Autopilot – ENGAGE AT 1,000' AGL
❏ Flaps – RETRACT TO 1 AT 1,000' AGL
❏ Flaps – UP AT 210 KIAS
❏ Autothrottle – OFF
❏ Thrust Levers – 90% N1
❏ Airspeed – 250 KIAS at 3,000' AGL
❏ Landing Gear Lever – VERIFY OFF

Date	Signature

Boeing 747-400

As the largest aircraft available in *Flight Simulator 2002*, the Boeing 747-400 offers you outstanding long-range ability, speed, and passenger capacity. It's been at the top of the class since its 1985 introduction for a reason! The 747 is truly an intercontinental aircraft, and its performance in this capacity is unmatched. Its size also makes it a true challenge to fly, especially if you're stepping into it straight from a Cessna 172. Performance is as solid as its manufacturer's name, and a 747 in the right hands can provide one of the smoothest rides in the skies.

Performance Data

V-SPEED	INDICATED AIRSPEED IN KNOTS
V1 – Takeoff Decision Speed	163 KIAS (880,000 lbs., flaps 10)
	158 KIAS (880,000 lbs., flaps 20)
VR – Rotation Speed	179 KIAS (880,000 lbs., flaps 10)
	173 KIAS (880,000 lbs., flaps 20)

Figure 2.5 *Boeing 747-400*

V-SPEED	INDICATED AIRSPEED IN KNOTS	
V2 – Takeoff Safety Speed	188 KIAS (880,000 lbs., flaps 10)	
	181 KIAS (880,000 lbs., flaps 20)	
Maximum Flap (Placard) Speeds	Flaps	KIAS
	1	280
	5	260
	10	240
	15	230
	25	205
	30	180
VLE – Maximum Landing Gear Extension (and Retraction) Speed	270 KIAS (.82 Mach)	
VLO – Maximum Gear Operating Speed	320 KIAS (.82 Mach)	

V-SPEED	INDICATED AIRSPEED IN KNOTS
VREF – Landing Approach Speed (flaps 30, gear down)	188 KIAS (850,000 lbs., flaps 25, gear down)
	181 KIAS (850,000 lbs., flaps 30, gear down)
	134 KIAS (450,000 lbs., flaps 25, gear down)
	129 KIAS (450,000 lbs., flaps 30, gear down)
VMO – Maximum Operating Speed (airspeed)	355 KIAS (.88 Mach)

TAKEOFF CHECKLIST
PLANE MODEL NAME (ALL VARIANTS)

Form Approved No. FS2002-0005

MS Department of Simulation
Sybex Aviation Administration

2. AIRCRAFT TAIL NUMBER

INSTRUCTIONS: *Personally complete all inspections prior to takeoff*

1. NAME *(Last, first, middle)*

3. DATE *(Month/Day/Year)*
/   /

4. FLIGHT INFORMATION

Point of Departure

Destination

INITIAL CHECKS

❏ Parking Brake – SET

ENGINE START-UP

❏ Ground Crew Assisted Start-Up – SIGNAL (Ctrl-E)

AFTER START

❏ De-Ice – AS REQUIRED

❏ Flight Controls – CHECK

❏ Autopilot – SET and OFF

❏ Instruments – CHECK

❏ Autobrake Switch – RTO

❏ Avionics Switch – ON

❏ Avionics – SET

❏ Trim – SET

❏ Beacon Light – ON
❏ Request Pushback – SIGNAL (Shift-P)

BEFORE TAKEOFF

❏ Flaps – SET FOR TAKEOFF (as necessary)
❏ Flight Director – ON
❏ Autothrottle – ARM (if using TO/GA mode for takeoff)

TAKEOFF

❏ Brakes – RELEASE
❏ Strobe Lights – ON
❏ Transponder – ALT
❏ Thrust Levers – ADVANCE TO 1.05 EPR
❏ Thrust Levers – ADVANCE SMOOTHLY TO 100% N1 -OR- TO/GA Mode – ENGAGE
❏ Engine Instruments – MONITOR
❏ Thrust Levers – VERIFY PROPER SETTING
❏ Airspeed 80 KIAS – CALL OUT *80 KNOTS*
❏ Airspeed V1 – CALL OUT *V1*
❏ Airspeed VR – CALL OUT *ROTATE*, ROTATE TO APPROX. 10 DEGREES PITCH UP
❏ Airspeed V2 – CALL OUT *V2*
❏ Landing Gear – RETRACT AFTER TAKEOFF
❏ Autopilot Heading Select Switch – ENGAGE IF DESIRED
❏ Airspeed – MAINTAIN V2+15 KIAS
❏ Autopilot – ENGAGE
❏ Flaps – START RETRACT ON SCHEDULE AT 1,000' AGL

Date	Signature

Boeing 777-300

Boeing's Triple Seven fills the need for intercontinental service on routes without a demand for high passenger capacity (where the 747 would be required). With its introduction in 1995, nonstop service between many international destinations became profitable, and a new era of direct air service was ushered in. The 777 is the first-ever aircraft to be designed entirely on computers, and this technical innovation is apparent from the cockpit to the cabin. This newfangled bird is the perfect choice for both international flights and for intercontinental routes between secondary airports.

Figure 2.6 *Boeing 777-300*

Performance Data

V-SPEED	INDICATED AIRSPEED IN KNOTS
V1 – Takeoff Decision Speed	155 KIAS (580,000 lbs.)
VR – Rotation Speed	158 KIAS (580,000 lbs., flaps 5)
V2 – Takeoff Safety Speed	163 KIAS (580,000 lbs., flaps 5)

V-SPEED	INDICATED AIRSPEED IN KNOTS	
Maximum Flap (Placard) Speeds	Flaps	KIAS
	1	255
	5	235
	15	215
	20	200
	25	190
	30	180
VLE – Maximum Landing Gear Extension Speed	270 KIAS/.82 Mach	
VLO – Maximum Gear Operating Speed	270 KIAS/.82 Mach	
VREF – Landing Approach Speed	157 KIAS (580,000 lbs., flaps 30, gear down)	

TAKEOFF CHECKLIST
PLANE MODEL NAME (ALL VARIANTS)

Form Approved No. FS2002-0006

MS Department of Simulation
Sybex Aviation Administration

2. AIRCRAFT TAIL NUMBER

INSTRUCTIONS: *Personally complete all inspections prior to takeoff*

1. NAME *(Last, first, middle)*

3. DATE *(Month/Day/Year)*

/   /

4. FLIGHT INFORMATION

Point of Departure

Destination

INITIAL CHECKS

❑ Parking Brake – SET

ENGINE START-UP

❑ Ground Crew Assisted Start-Up – SIGNAL (Ctrl-E)

AFTER START

❑ De-Ice – AS REQUIRED

❑ Flight Controls – CHECK

❑ Autopilot – SET and OFF

❑ Instruments – CHECK

❑ Autobrake Switch – RTO

❏ Avionics Switch – ON
❏ Avionics – SET
❏ Trim – SET
❏ Beacon Light – ON
❏ Request Pushback – SIGNAL (Shift-P)

BEFORE TAKEOFF

❏ Flaps – SET FOR TAKEOFF (as necessary)
❏ Flight Director – ON
❏ Autothrottle – ARM (if using TO/GA mode for takeoff)

TAKEOFF

❏ Brakes – RELEASE
❏ Strobe Lights – ON
❏ Transponder – ALT
❏ Thrust Levers – ADVANCE TO 1.05 EPR
❏ Thrust Levers – ADVANCE SMOOTHLY TO 100% N1 -OR- TO/GA Mode – ENGAGE
❏ Thrust Levers – VERIFY PROPER SETTING
❏ Airspeed 80 KIAS – CALL OUT *80 KNOTS*
❏ Airspeed V1 – CALL OUT *V1*
❏ Airspeed VR – CALL OUT *ROTATE*, ROTATE TO APPROX. 10 DEGREES PITCH UP
❏ Airspeed V2 – CALL OUT *V2*
❏ Landing Gear – RETRACT AFTER TAKEOFF
❏ Autopilot Heading Select Switch – ENGAGE IF DESIRED
❏ Airspeed – MAINTAIN V2+15 KIAS
❏ Autopilot – ENGAGE
❏ Flaps – START RETRACT ON SCHEDULE AT 1,000' AGL

Date	Signature

Cessna

The Cessna Aircraft Corporation enjoys the Holy Grail of marketing—its brand name is synonymous with its product. Many people casually refer to all light aircraft as "Cessnas," just as they might casually request a Kleenex even when they really don't care what brand of facial tissue you hand them. In any case, the name recognition is well deserved in this case, as the single-engine Cessnas are collectively the world's best-selling aircraft of any type.

Cessna 172SP Skyhawk

Nearly every pilot in the world has logged a few hours on a Cessna 172. These standbys are unmatched in what they do, providing consistent, stable aircraft for personal or business use. The Skyhawk's easy handling makes it the perfect choice for novice pilots just earning their wings, while its dependability, economy, and respectable range make it well suited for excursion flights, vacation or commuter transportation, and short business runs.

Figure 2.7 *Cessna 172SP Skyhawk*

Performance Data

V-SPEED	INDICATED AIRSPEED IN KNOTS
VA – Maneuvering Speed	105 KIAS (2,550 lbs.)
	98 KIAS (2,200 lbs.)
	90 KIAS (1,900 lbs.)

V-SPEED	INDICATED AIRSPEED IN KNOTS
VSO – Stalling Speed in the Landing Configuration	40 KIAS (maximum weight, flaps 30)
VS – Stalling Speed	48 KIAS (maximum weight, flaps up)
VNE – Never Exceed Speed	163 KIAS
VFE – Maximum Flaps Extended Speed	110 KIAS (flaps 10)
	85 KIAS (flaps 10–30)
VNO – Maximum Structural-Cruising Speed	129 KIAS
VX – Best Angle-of-Climb Speed	62 KIAS (sea level)
	67 KIAS (10,000' MSL)
VY – Best Rate-of-Climb Speed	74 KIAS (sea level)
	72 KIAS (10,000' MSL)
Maximum Glide Range Speed	68 KIAS

TAKEOFF CHECKLIST
PLANE MODEL NAME (ALL VARIANTS)

Form Approved No. FS2002-0007

MS Department of Simulation
Sybex Aviation Administration

2. AIRCRAFT TAIL NUMBER

INSTRUCTIONS: *Personally complete all inspections prior to takeoff*

1. NAME *(Last, first, middle)*

3. DATE *(Month/Day/Year)*
/   /

4. FLIGHT INFORMATION

Point of Departure

Destination

INITIAL CHECKS

❏ Brakes – TEST and SET

❏ Electrical Equipment, Autopilot – OFF

❏ Avionics Master Switch – OFF

❏ Fuel Selector Valve – BOTH

ENGINE START-UP

- ❏ Throttle – OPEN 1/4 INCH
- ❏ Mixture – RICH
- ❏ Propeller Area – CHECK CLEAR
- ❏ Master Switch – ON
- ❏ Auxiliary Fuel Pump Switch – ON
- ❏ Ignition Switch – START (release when engine starts)
- ❏ Oil Pressure – CHECK
- ❏ Auxiliary Fuel Pump Switch – OFF
- ❏ Beacon and Nav Lights – AS REQUIRED
- ❏ Avionics Master Switch – ON
- ❏ Flaps – RETRACT

BEFORE TAXI

- ❏ Parking Brake – SET
- ❏ Flight Controls – FREE AND CORRECT
- ❏ Flight Instruments – CHECK and SET
- ❏ Fuel Quantity – CHECK
- ❏ Mixture – RICH
- ❏ Fuel Selector Valve – CHECK BOTH
- ❏ Elevator Trim Tabs – SET
- ❏ Avionics – CHECK
- ❏ Autopilot – CHECK
- ❏ Electronic Pitch Trim Control – CHECK
- ❏ Throttle – 1800 RPM
- ❏ Magnetos – CHECK (click each to L, R, L, Both, look for <150 RPM drop on each, <50 RPM drop between)
- ❏ Suction Gauge – CHECK
- ❏ Engine Instruments and Ammeter – CHECK
- ❏ Annunciator Panel – CHECK (Shift-4)
- ❏ Throttle – <1000 RPM
- ❏ Strobe Lights – AS DESIRED

❏ Radio and Avionics – ST
❏ Autopilot – OFF
❏ Flaps – SET for takeoff (0–10 degrees)
❏ Brakes – RELEASE
TAKEOFF
❏ Wing Flaps – 0–10 degrees
❏ Throttle – FULL OPEN
❏ Mixture – RICH (above 3,000' MSL, LEAN to achieve maximum RPM)
❏ Airspeed – ROTATE AT Vr (approx. 55 knots)
❏ Airspeed – MAINTAIN V2 (70–80 KIAS)
❏ Flaps – UP

Date	Signature

Cessna 182 Skylane (All Models)

The Skylane is the stronger, faster brother of the Skyhawk. With more robust performance and longer range, the 182 is a step up from the 172. However, the aircraft is more complex and is not as forgiving as its gentler stablemate. The "RG" model in *Flight Simulator 2002*

Figure 2.8 *Cessna 182RG Skylane*

has retractable landing gear, which allow for higher cruise speeds. Use the Skylane to learn and practice IFR (Instrument Flight Rules) procedures and as a transition between more complex aircraft such as the Mooney and Baron and the Skyhawk.

Performance Data

V-SPEED	INDICATED AIRSPEED IN KNOTS
VA – Maneuvering Speed	112 KIAS (3,100 lbs.)
	101 KIAS (2,550 lbs.)
	89 KIAS (2,000 lbs.)
VSO – Stalling Speed in the Landing Configuration	39 KIAS (maximum weight, forward CG)
VS – Stalling Speed	41 KIAS (maximum weight, forward CG)
VNE – Never Exceed Speed	181 KIAS
VFE – Maximum Flaps Extended Speed	140 KIAS (flaps 0–10)
	120 KIAS (flaps 10–20)
	95 KIAS (flaps 20–full)
VNO – Maximum Structural Cruising Speed	159 KIAS
VX – Best Angle-of-Climb Speed	65 KIAS (sea level)
	67 KIAS (10,000')
VY – Best Rate-of-Climb Speed	88 KIAS (sea level)
	75 KIAS (10,000')
Maximum Glide Range Speed	80 KIAS (3,100 lbs.)
	72 KIAS (2,550 lbs.)
	64 KIAS (2,000 lbs.)
VLE – Maximum Landing Gear Extension Speed	140 KIAS
VLO – Maximum Gear Operating Speed	140 KIAS

Cessna

TAKEOFF CHECKLIST
PLANE MODEL NAME (ALL VARIANTS)

MS Department of Simulation
Sybex Aviation Administration

Form Approved No. FS2002-0008

2. AIRCRAFT TAIL NUMBER

INSTRUCTIONS: *Personally complete all inspections prior to takeoff*

1. NAME *(Last, first, middle)*

3. DATE *(Month/Day/Year)*
/   /

4. FLIGHT INFORMATION

Point of Departure

Destination

INITIAL CHECKS

- ❏ Brakes – TEST and SET
- ❏ Electrical Equipment – OFF
- ❏ Avionics Power Switch – OFF
- ❏ Landing Gear Lever – DOWN
- ❏ Cowl Flaps – OPEN
- ❏ Fuel Selector Valve – BOTH

ENGINE START-UP

- ❏ Prime – AS REQUIRED
- ❏ Throttle – PUMP ONCE, then OPEN 1/4 INCH
- ❏ Propeller – HIGH RPM
- ❏ Mixture – RICH
- ❏ Propeller Area – CHECK CLEAR
- ❏ Master Switch – ON
- ❏ Ignition Switch – START (release when engine starts)
- ❏ Oil Pressure – CHECK
- ❏ Avionics Power Switch – ON
- ❏ Beacon and Nav Lights – AS REQUIRED
- ❏ Flaps – RETRACT

BEFORE TAXI

- ❏ Parking Brake – SET
- ❏ Flight Controls – FREE AND CORRECT

❏ Flight Instruments – CHECK and SET

❏ Primer – LOCKED

❏ Fuel Quantity – CHECK

❏ Mixture – RICH

❏ Fuel Selector Valve – CHECK BOTH

❏ Trim Tabs – SET

❏ Avionics – CHECK

❏ Autopilot – CHECK

❏ Electronic Pitch Trim Control – CHECK

❏ Throttle – 1700 RPM

❏ Magnetos – CHECK (click each to L, R, L, Both, look for <150 RPM drop on each, <50 RPM drop between)

❏ Carburetor Heat – CHECK (look for RPM drop when engaged)

❏ Propeller – CYCLE high/low/high RPM

❏ Vacuum Gauge – CHECK

❏ Engine Instruments and Ammeter – CHECK

❏ Throttle – 800–1000 RPM

❏ Strobe Lights – AS DESIRED

❏ Radio and Avionics – ST

❏ Autopilot – OFF

❏ Flaps – SET for takeoff (0–20 degrees)

❏ Cowl Flaps – OPEN

❏ Brakes – RELEASE

TAKEOFF

❏ Flaps – 0–20 degrees

❏ Carburetor Heat – COLD

❏ Mixture – RICH (above 3,000' MSL, LEAN to achieve maximum RPM)

❏ Propeller – 2400 RPM

❏ Throttle – FULL OPEN

❏ Airspeed – ROTATE AT Vr (approx. 50 knots)

❏ Airspeed – MAINTAIN CLIMB SPEED

❑ Brakes – APPLY MOMENTARILY	
❑ Landing Gear – RETRACT AFTER TAKEOFF	
❑ Flaps – RETRACT	
Date	**Signature**

Cessna 208B Caravan (All Models)

A true workhorse in every sense of the word, the Caravan is a top-of-the-line Cessna. With extremely robust construction, reinforced landing gear, an amphibian option, and ample cargo and fuel capacity, the Caravan can go just about anywhere an airplane can go. If you're looking to take a large cargo to a remote spot, this is the natural choice.

Figure 2.9 *Cessna 208B Caravan*

Performance Data

V-SPEED	INDICATED AIRSPEED IN KNOTS
VR – Rotation Speed	70–75 KIAS
VSO – Stalling Speed in the Landing Configuration	50 KIAS (flaps 30)
VS – Stalling Speed	63 KIAS (flaps up)
VMO – Maximum Operating Speed	175 KIAS

V-SPEED	INDICATED AIRSPEED IN KNOTS
VFE – Maximum Flaps Extended Speed	175 KIAS (flaps to 10 degrees)
	150 KIAS (flaps 10–20)
	125 KIAS (flaps 20–30)
Landing Approach Speed	100–115 KIAS (flaps up)
	75–85 KIAS (flaps 30)
VX – Best Angle-of-Climb Speed	72 KIAS
VY – Best Rate-of-Climb Speed	104 KIAS (sea level to 10,000' MSL)
	87 KIAS (20,000' MSL)
Cruise Climb	110–120 KIAS
Maximum Glide Range Speed (with cargo pod)	95 KIAS (8,750 lbs.)
	87 KIAS (7,500 lbs.)
	79 KIAS (6,250 lbs.)
	71 KIAS (5,000 lbs.)

TAKEOFF CHECKLIST
PLANE MODEL NAME (ALL VARIANTS)

Form Approved No. FS2002-0009

MS Department of Simulation
Sybex Aviation Administration

2. AIRCRAFT TAIL NUMBER

INSTRUCTIONS: *Personally complete all inspections prior to takeoff*

1. NAME *(Last, first, middle)*

3. DATE *(Month/Day/Year)*
/   /

4. FLIGHT INFORMATION

Point of Departure	Destination

INITIAL CHECKS

❏ Brakes – TEST and SET

❏ Switches – OFF

❏ Fuel Selector Valve – BOTH

❏ Emergency Power Lever – NORMAL

❏ Power Lever – IDLE

❏ Propeller Control Lever – MAX

❏ Fuel Condition Lever – CUTOFF

❏ Fuel Shutoff – ON

❏ Battery Switch – ON

❏ Flaps – UP

ENGINE START-UP

❏ Battery Switch – ON

❏ Emergency Power Lever – NORMAL

❏ Propeller Area – CHECK CLEAR

❏ Fuel Boost Switch – ON

❏ *AUX FUEL PUMP ON* Annunciator – CHECK ON (Shift-5)

❏ No Fuel Flow – CONFIRM

❏ Starter Switch – START (release when engine starts)

❏ *IGNITION ON* Annunciator – CHECK ON (Shift-5)

❏ Engine Oil Pressure – CHECK

❏ Ng – STABLE (12% MINIMUM)

❏ Fuel Condition Lever – LOW IDLE

❏ Fuel Flow – CHECK for 80 to 110 pph

❏ ITT – MONITOR (1,090 degrees C max)

❏ Ng – 52% MINIMUM

❏ Starter Switch – OFF

❏ *STARTER ENERGIZED* Annunciator – CHECK OFF

❏ Engine Instruments – CHECK

❏ *GENERATOR OFF* Annunciator – CHECK OFF

❏ Fuel Boost Switch – NORM

❏ *AUX FUEL PUMP ON* Annunciator – CHECK OFF

❏ Avionics Master Switch – ON

❏ Beacon and Nav Lights – AS REQUIRED

❏ Suction Gauge – CHECK

❏ Radios – AS REQUIRED

BEFORE TAXI

❏ Parking Brake – SET

❏ Flight Controls – FREE AND CORRECT

❏ Flight Instruments – CHECK and SET
❏ Fuel Boost Switch – CHECK NORM
❏ Fuel Tank Selector – CHECK BOTH
❏ Fuel Quantity – CHECK
❏ Fuel Shutoff – CHECK FULLY ON
❏ Trim Tabs – SET
❏ Power Lever – 400 FT-LBS
❏ Suction Gauge – CHECK
❏ *VOLTAGE LOW* Annunciator – CHECK OFF
❏ Inertial Separator – CHECK
❏ Engine Instruments – CHECK
❏ Overspeed Governor – CHECK (stabilized at 1750/60 RPM)
❏ Power Lever – IDLE
❏ Pitot Static Heat – ON when ambient temp is below 4 degrees C
❏ Ice Protection – AS REQUIRED
❏ Avionics – CHECK AND SET
❏ GPS/NAV Switch – SET
❏ Strobe Lights – AS REQUIRED
❏ Annunciators – EXTINGUISHED OR CONSIDERED
❏ Flaps – SET AT 20 DEGREES
❏ Brakes – RELEASE
❏ Fuel Condition Lever – HIGH IDLE

TAKEOFF

❏ Flaps – 20 degrees
❏ Power – SET FOR TAKEOFF (1900 RPM)
❏ Annunciators – EXTINGUISHED OR CONSIDERED
❏ Airspeed – ROTATE AT Vr (approx. 70–75 knots)
❏ Airspeed – MAINTAIN CLIMB SPEED (approx. 85–95 knots)
❏ Flaps – RETRACT TO 10 DEGREES AT 85 KIAS AND 0 DEGREES AT 95 KIAS

Date	**Signature**

Extra

Extra is more than just the catchy name of a hot plane—there really is a Walter Extra! His personal experience with aerobatic competitions led him to design his own plane in 1982, and the Extra has become synonymous with speed, power, and agility in the nearly two decades since its debut.

Extra 300S

The Extra 300S is the single-seat version of the 300 Series unlimited class of aerobatic monoplanes. Certified at a staggering +/- 10 Gs, the Extra 300s is truly an incredible performer. Chapter 4: Spreading Your Wings teaches you how to take the Extra to the very edge of flight. Whenever you're itching to loop, roll, and zip your way through the air, the Extra 300s is waiting for you.

Figure 2.10 *Extra 300S*

Performance Data

V-SPEED	INDICATED AIRSPEED IN KNOTS
VA – Maneuvering Speed	140 KIAS (normal)
	158 KIAS (aerobatic)
VNE – Never Exceed Speed	220 KIAS

V-SPEED	INDICATED AIRSPEED IN KNOTS
VS – Stalling Speed	59 KIAS (normal, forward CG)
	55 KIAS (aerobatic, forward CG)
VNO – Maximum Structural Cruising Speed	158 KIAS
VX – Best Angle-of-Climb Speed	93 KIAS (normal)
	87 KIAS (aerobatic)
VY – Best Rate-of-Climb Speed	104 KIAS (normal)
	96 KIAS (aerobatic)
Best Glide Speed	90 KIAS (normal)
	80 KIAS (aerobatic)
Load Factor Limitations	+6 G/-3 G (normal)
	+10 G/-10 G (aerobatic)

Recommended Aerobatic Maneuver Entry Speeds

MANEUVER	MINIMUM ENTRY SPEED	MAXIMUM ENTRY SPEED
Horizontal Line	VS	VNO
45-Degree Climbing	80 KIAS	VNO
90-Degree Up	158 KIAS	VNO
45-Degree Diving	VS	VNO
90-Degree Diving	VS	VNO
1/4 Loop Climb	100 KIAS	190 KIAS
Looping	100 KIAS	190 KIAS
Stall Turn	100 KIAS	190 KIAS
Aileron Roll	80 KIAS	158 KIAS
Snap Roll	80 KIAS	140 KIAS
Tail Slide	100 KIAS	190 KIAS
Spin	VS	VNE
Knife Edge	150 KIAS	VNE
Inverted Flight	VS	190 KIAS

TAKEOFF CHECKLIST
PLANE MODEL NAME (ALL VARIANTS)

MS Department of Simulation
Sybex Aviation Administration

Form Approved No. FS2002-0010

2. AIRCRAFT TAIL NUMBER

INSTRUCTIONS: *Personally complete all inspections prior to takeoff*

1. NAME *(Last, first, middle)*

3. DATE *(Month/Day/Year)*
/   /

4. FLIGHT INFORMATION

Point of Departure

Destination

INITIAL CHECKS

- ❏ Brakes – TEST and SET
- ❏ Master Switch – ON
- ❏ Avionics Master Switch – OFF
- ❏ Electrical Equipment – OFF
- ❏ Alternator – ON
- ❏ Nav/Strobe Lights – ON

ENGINE START-UP

- ❏ Propeller – HIGH RPM
- ❏ Mixture – RICH
- ❏ Throttle – OPEN 1/4 TRAVEL
- ❏ Boost Pump – ON
- ❏ Propeller Area – CHECK CLEAR
- ❏ Ignition Switch – START (release when engine starts)
- ❏ Boost Pump – OFF
- ❏ Oil Pressure – CHECK
- ❏ Avionics Master Switch – ON

BEFORE TAXI

- ❏ Parking Brake – SET
- ❏ Flight Controls – FREE AND CORRECT
- ❏ Flight Instruments – CHECK and SET
- ❏ Oil Pressure – CHECK
- ❏ Mixture – CHECK RICH

❏ Fuel Quantity – CHECK
❏ Throttle – 1800 RPM
❏ Magnetos – CHECK (click each to L, R, L, Both, look for <175 RPM drop on each, <50 RPM drop between)
❏ Propeller – CYCLE high/low/high RPM
❏ Boost Pump – ON (check fuel flow)
❏ Engine Instruments and Ammeter – CHECK
❏ Throttle – 800–1000 RPM
❏ Strobe Lights – AS DESIRED
❏ Avionics Master Switch – CHECK ON
❏ Radio and Avionics – ST
❏ Brakes – RELEASE
TAKEOFF
❏ Mixture – RICH (above 3,000' MSL, LEAN to achieve maximum RPM)
❏ Propeller – HIGH RPM
❏ Throttle – FULL OPEN
❏ Elevator Control – GENTLY PUSH FORWARD ON STICK UNTIL TAIL COMES UP
❏ Propeller – 2400 RPM
❏ Airspeed – ROTATE AT Vr
❏ Airspeed – MAINTAIN CLIMB SPEED (approx. 100 KIAS)
❏ Boost Pump – OFF

Date	Signature

Learjet

Learjet is the leading manufacturer of business jets. Its name recognition is unrivaled in the executive jet market. Most Learjet designs are associated with speed and performance above all things. *Flight Simulator 2002* affords you the opportunity to fly the latest Learjet, the Model 45.

Learjet Model 45

Designed entirely on computers, the Model 45 is a precise aircraft in every way. It can easily cruise at 45,000 feet and can do so at a whopping 445 knots—which puts it in the same league as commercial airliners! Choose the Learjet whenever you have time-sensitive or VIP passengers. The Learjet's high service ceiling makes it a good choice on stormy days, as you can climb over the weather for a smooth ride above the clouds.

Figure 2.11 *Learjet 45*

Performance Data

V-SPEED	INDICATED AIRSPEED IN KNOTS
V1 – Takeoff Decision Speed	107 KIAS (for all conditions, with anti-skid off)
V2 – Takeoff Safety Speed	120 KIAS (13,000 lbs.)
	130 KIAS (20,200 lbs.)
VR – Rotation Speed	108 KIAS (13,000 lbs.)
	119 KIAS (20,200 lbs.)

V-SPEED	INDICATED AIRSPEED IN KNOTS
VA – Maneuvering Speed	12,500 lbs.
	150 KIAS (sea level)
	163 KIAS (20,000')
	195 KIAS (40,000')
	20,200 lbs.
	198 KIAS (sea level)
	225 KIAS (20,000')
	245 KIAS (40,000')
VMO – Maximum Operating Speed	330 KIAS
VFE – Maximum Flaps Extended Speed	250 KIAS (flaps 8)
	200 KIAS (flaps 20)
	150 KIAS (flaps 40)
VLE – Maximum Landing Gear Extension Speed	260 KIAS
VLO – Maximum Gear Operating Speed	200 KIAS
Maximum Glide Range Speed	160 KIAS (gear and flaps up)
VREF – Landing Approach Speed	103 KIAS (13,000 lbs., flaps 40, gear down)
	123 KIAS (19,200 lbs., flaps 40, gear down)

TAKEOFF CHECKLIST
PLANE MODEL NAME (ALL VARIANTS)

Form Approved No. FS2002-0011

MS Department of Simulation
Sybex Aviation Administration

2. AIRCRAFT TAIL NUMBER

INSTRUCTIONS: *Personally complete all inspections prior to takeoff*

1. NAME *(Last, first, middle)*

3. DATE *(Month/Day/Year)*

/   /

4. FLIGHT INFORMATION

Point of Departure

Destination

INITIAL CHECKS

❏ Gear – CHECK DOWN

❏ BATT Switch – ON

❏ L and R GEN Switches – OFF

❏ Flight Controls – CHECK

❏ Engine Instruments – CHECK

❏ Fuel Quantity – CHECK

❏ De-Ice – OFF

❏ Aircraft Lighting – OFF

❏ Parking Brake – SET

❏ Trim – AS DESIRED

❏ Altimeters – SET

❏ Standby Instruments – SET

❏ Takeoff Data (V1, VR, V2) – COMPUTED and SPEEDS SET

❏ Avionics Master Switch – ON

❏ Avionics – SET FOR DEPARTURE

ENGINE START-UP

❏ Beacon/Strobe Switch – BCN/STROBE

❏ Parking Brake – SET

❏ Thrust Levers – IDLE

❏ Fuel Flow – ON

❏ L Start Switch – ON (release after engine start)

❏ L Fuel Flow – CHECK

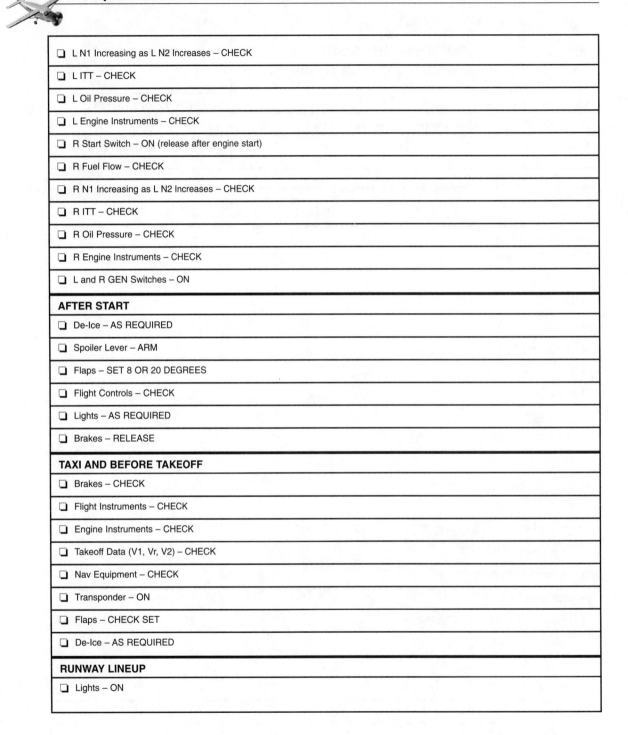

❏ L N1 Increasing as L N2 Increases – CHECK

❏ L ITT – CHECK

❏ L Oil Pressure – CHECK

❏ L Engine Instruments – CHECK

❏ R Start Switch – ON (release after engine start)

❏ R Fuel Flow – CHECK

❏ R N1 Increasing as L N2 Increases – CHECK

❏ R ITT – CHECK

❏ R Oil Pressure – CHECK

❏ R Engine Instruments – CHECK

❏ L and R GEN Switches – ON

AFTER START

❏ De-Ice – AS REQUIRED

❏ Spoiler Lever – ARM

❏ Flaps – SET 8 OR 20 DEGREES

❏ Flight Controls – CHECK

❏ Lights – AS REQUIRED

❏ Brakes – RELEASE

TAXI AND BEFORE TAKEOFF

❏ Brakes – CHECK

❏ Flight Instruments – CHECK

❏ Engine Instruments – CHECK

❏ Takeoff Data (V1, Vr, V2) – CHECK

❏ Nav Equipment – CHECK

❏ Transponder – ON

❏ Flaps – CHECK SET

❏ De-Ice – AS REQUIRED

RUNWAY LINEUP

❏ Lights – ON

TAKEOFF
❏ Thrust Lever – T/O
❏ Brakes – RELEASE
❏ Airspeed VR – ROTATE TO APPROX. 10 DEGREES PITCH UP
❏ Landing Gear – RETRACT AFTER TAKEOFF
❏ Flaps – UP AT V2+25 KIAS
❏ Yaw Damper – ON AS REQUIRED
❏ Spoiler Lever – RET
❏ De-Ice – AS REQUIRED
❏ L and R LDG-TAXI Light Switches – OFF

Date	Signature

Mooney

Despite a troubled beginning plagued by financial troubles and questionable management decisions in the first part of the 20th century, Mooney has earned a reputation as a reliable manufacturer of excellent light civil aircraft. Immediately recognizable by their strong lines and forward-swept vertical stabilizers, Mooney aircraft are regarded as attractive, sleek, and of very high quality.

Figure 2.12 *Mooney Bravo*

Mooney Bravo

The Mooney Bravo is the sports car of civil aviation. Its big Lycoming engine delivers an impressive 270 horsepower, propelling the aircraft to hold the record as the fastest single-engine civil airplane currently in production. The turbocharger increases its high-altitude performance, and in fact above 10,000 feet the Mooney can outrun most twin-engine light aircraft! A respectable service ceiling is enough to get you over most threatening weather, while the engine gets you quickly past whatever you can't avoid. For any private pilot who values speed, the Mooney Bravo is the plane to fly.

Performance Data

V-SPEED	INDICATED AIRSPEED IN KNOTS
VA – Maneuvering Speed	127 KIAS (3,368 lbs.)
	123 KIAS (3,200 lbs.)
	117 KIAS (2,900 lbs.)
	111 KIAS (2,600 lbs.)
VS – Stalling Speed	66 KIAS (maximum weight, forward CG)
VSO – Stalling Speed in the Landing Configuration	59 KIAS
VNO – Maximum Structural Cruising Speed	174 KIAS
VNE – Never Exceed Speed	195 KIAS
VFE – Maximum Flaps Extended Speed	110 KIAS (flaps fully down)
VLE – Maximum Landing Gear Extension Speed	165 KIAS
VLO – Maximum Gear Operating Speed	140 KIAS (extension)
	106 KIAS (retraction)
Maximum Glide Range Speed	93.5 KIAS (3,368 lbs.)
	89 KIAS (3,200 lbs.)
	84.5 KIAS (2,900 lbs.)
	80 KIAS (2,600 lbs.)
VX – Best Angle-of-Climb Speed	85 KIAS
VY – Best Rate-of-Climb Speed	105 KIAS

TAKEOFF CHECKLIST
PLANE MODEL NAME (ALL VARIANTS)

MS Department of Simulation
Sybex Aviation Administration

Form Approved No. FS2002-0012

2. AIRCRAFT TAIL NUMBER

INSTRUCTIONS: *Personally complete all inspections prior to takeoff*

1. NAME *(Last, first, middle)*

3. DATE *(Month/Day/Year)*
/   /

4. FLIGHT INFORMATION

Point of Departure

Destination

INITIAL CHECKS

❏ Magneto/Starter Switch – OFF

❏ Master Switch – OFF

❏ Fuel Boost Pump Switch – OFF

❏ Throttle – CLOSED

❏ Propeller – HIGH RPM

❏ Mixture – IDLE CUTOFF

❏ Parking Brakes – SET

❏ Master Switch – ON

❏ Cowl Flaps – OPEN

❏ Flaps – Up

❏ Master Switch – OFF

❏ Landing Gear Switch – DOWN

ENGINE START-UP

❏ Throttle – OPEN 1/4 INCH

❏ Propeller – HIGH RPM

❏ Mixture – RICH

❏ Master Switch – ON

❏ Fuel Boost Pump Switch – ON for 0–40 SECONDS (depending on temperature)

❏ Fuel Boost Pump Switch – OFF

❏ Propeller Area – CHECK CLEAR

❏ Magneto/Starter Switch – START (release when engine starts)

❏ Throttle – IDLE (700–750 RPM)

❏ Oil Pressure – CHECK
❏ Ammeter – CHECK
❏ Engine Instruments – CHECK
BEFORE TAXI
❏ Parking Brake – SET
❏ Avionics Master Switch – ON
❏ Heading Indicator – SET
❏ Instruments – NORMAL OPERATION
❏ Radios and Avionics – CHECK and SET
❏ Altimeter – SET
❏ Fuel Selector Valve – CHECK BOTH TANKS
❏ Cowl Flaps – FULL OPEN
❏ Fuel Selector Valve – FULLEST TANK
❏ Throttle – 1000 RPM
❏ Mixture – RICH
❏ Alternator Switch – VERIFY ON
❏ Throttle – 2000 RPM
❏ Magnetos – CHECK (click each to L, R, L, Both, look for <150 RPM drop on each, <50 RPM drop between)
❏ Propeller – CYCLE high/low/high RPM
❏ Ammeter – CHECK positive charge indication
❏ Throttle – 1000 RPM
❏ Fuel Pump Boost Switch – ON (verify annunciator lit)
❏ Trim Tabs – SET
❏ Flaps – SET AT 10 DEGREES
❏ Flight Controls – FREE AND CORRECT
❏ Radio and Avionics – SET
❏ Annunciator Panel – CHECK (Shift-4)
❏ Strobe Lights/Beacon – ON
❏ Oil Temperature – CHECK
❏ Cylinder Head Temperature – CHECK

❏ Brakes – RELEASE
TAXI
❏ Rudder Trim – AS DESIRED
❏ Parking Brake – RELEASE
❏ Brakes – CHECK
❏ Directional Gyro – PROPER INDICATION during turns
❏ Turn Coordinator – PROPER INDICATION during turns
❏ Artificial Horizon – ERECT during turns
❏ Throttle – MINIMUM POWER
❏ Cowl Flaps – OPEN
❏ Propeller – HIGH RPM
TAKEOFF
❏ Throttle – FULL
❏ Annunciator Panel – CHECK (Shift-4)
❏ Lights – AS DESIRED
❏ Engine Instruments – CHECK
❏ Airspeed – ROTATE AT Vr (approx. 60 knots)
❏ Airspeed – MAINTAIN V2 (approx. 85 KIAS)
❏ Landing Gear – RETRACT AFTER TAKEOFF
❏ Flaps – UP

Date	Signature

Schweizer

Schweizer is a diversified presence in the aerospace industry, working as a subcontractor manufacturing parts for other aircraft companies. This helped the company remain profitable even when sailplanes weren't the best business to be in. That was good news for sailplane enthusiasts around the world, as Schweizer Aircraft Company managed to endure long enough to produce the SGS 2-32. The high-performance sailplane remains popular even now, over a quarter of a century after its introduction.

Schweizer SGS 2-32 Sailplane

The SGS 2-32 is an American-made sailplane built entirely around performance, longevity, and quality. With a 1:36 glide ratio, this all-metal sailplane was the natural choice for one of the first attempts at a nonstop flight around the world. It eventually set the record at an amazing 8,974 miles with the help of a small engine. The Schweizer is obviously one of a kind in *Flight Simulator 2002*, perfect for those days when you don't want to hear anything except the rush of the wind across your canopy.

Figure 2.13 *Schweizer SGS 2-32 Sailplane*

Performance Data

V-SPEED	INDICATED AIRSPEED IN MPH
Maximum Glide Speed	158 MPH IAS (dive brakes open)
	150 MPH IAS (dive brakes closed)
Minimum Sink Speed	54 MPH IAS
VSO – Stall Speed	47 MPH IAS
Optimal Speed for Spiraling in Thermals	58 MPH IAS (30-degree bank)
	60 MPH IAS (45-degree bank)
Maximum Glide Range Speed	64 MPH IAS

Takeoff Checklist

Since you can't "take off" in a sailplane, there's no checklist to go through! You must use the slew feature to "tow" your plane to the desired launch point. Use the joystick or numeric keypad to move across the countryside, and F4 and F1 to change your altitude. Get up to about 4,000 feet, and then press "Y" to start your flight.

Sopwith

Thomas Sopwith was the 32nd pilot to earn a flight certification from the British government. After competing in flying competitions throughout Great Britain and Europe, he set about designing and building his own aircraft. The Sopwith Aviation Company eventually went on to manufacture several of the aircraft that formed the backbone of the Royal Flying Corps in the First World War, including the Pup, the Sopwith Triplane, and the legendary Camel.

Sopwith 2F.1 Camel

Constructed almost entirely out of wood and canvas, the Sopwith Camel is a nostalgic look into the dawn of flight. At the time of its introduction in 1917, the Camel was one of the deadliest planes in the air, with a high top speed, excellent maneuverability, and two powerful machine guns. The agility came at a price, however, as the plane was extremely nose-

Figure 2.14 *Sopwith 2F.1 Camel*

heavy. If you are looking for a flight into history, do so with a light touch—the Camel can easily maneuver outside of its flight envelope, potentially bringing the antique crashing to the earth. If you're gentle, however, there's nothing to compare with the feeling of flying in the Camel's open cockpit, just as the brave airmen of the Great War did so long ago.

Performance Data

V-SPEED	INDICATED AIRSPEED IN MPH
VNE – Never Exceed Speed	160 MPH IAS
VS – Stall Speed	35 MPH IAS

TAKEOFF CHECKLIST PLANE MODEL NAME (ALL VARIANTS)		Form Approved No. FS2002-0013
MS Department of Simulation **Sybex Aviation Administration**		**2. AIRCRAFT TAIL NUMBER**
INSTRUCTIONS: *Personally complete all inspections prior to takeoff*		
1. NAME *(Last, first, middle)*		**3. DATE** *(Month/Day/Year)* / /
4. FLIGHT INFORMATION		
Point of Departure	Destination	
INITIAL CHECKS		
❏ Parking Brake – SET		
❏ Magneto Switches – BOTH OFF		
❏ Fuel Gauge – CHECK QUANTITY INDICATED		
ENGINE START-UP		
❏ Throttle – OPEN 1/4 INCH		
❏ Propeller Area – CHECK CLEAR		
❏ Magneto Switches – BOTH ON		
❏ Ground Crew Start – SIGNAL (Ctrl-E)		
❏ Throttle – IDLE (700–750 RPM)		
❏ Oil Pressure – CHECK		

BEFORE TAXI

❏ Parking Brake – SET

❏ Instruments – NORMAL OPERATION

❏ Radios and Avionics – CHECK and SET

❏ Altimeter – SET

❏ Throttle – 2000 RPM

❏ Magnetos – CHECK (click each to verify individual operation)

❏ Oil Pressure – MONITOR

❏ Throttle – 1000 RPM

❏ Flight Controls – FREE AND CORRECT

❏ Radio – SET

❏ Brakes – RELEASE

TAXI

❏ Trim Tabs – AS DESIRED

❏ Parking Brake – RELEASE

❏ Brakes – CHECK

TAKEOFF

❏ Throttle – FULL

❏ Oil Pressure – CHECK

❏ Elevator Control – GENTLY PUSH FORWARD ON STICK UNTIL TAIL COMES UP

❏ Airspeed – ROTATE AT Vr (approx. 55 knots)

❏ Airspeed – MAINTAIN V2 (60 KIAS or greater)

Date	Signature
.	

CHAPTER 3
Navigation

Aircraft are a mode of transportation, and transportation means getting from one place to another. But there are no roads or road signs, no gas stations at which to ask directions, and no exit ramps in the sky. Without familiar navigational aids, finding your way from point A to point B can be a serious consideration. Worse yet, everything looks different from the air, so it's not a simple matter of knowing the way to Grandma's house, either.

This chapter explains the sky's highways. It also provides a look at Visual Flight Rules and Instrument Flight Rules navigation, so you can fly the Flight Simulator 2002 skies accurately and safely.

Airspace

Just because there aren't any signs or paved roads doesn't mean that there aren't established (and enforced!) highways in the sky. Indeed, just about every square inch of airspace in the civilized world is controlled, categorized, or classified by a governing agency of some kind. Each type of airspace is classified for a specific reason: traffic density, airport operations, military training, or a number of other uses (see Figure 3.1). The penalties for entering a class of airspace improperly are severe, ranging from a warning from air traffic control to the revocation of your pilot's license by the Federal Aviation Administration (FAA), or even being shot down by military forces.

Figure 3.1 *All air looks the same, but this plane has just crossed a boundary into Class B airspace.*

Since these penalties are potentially severe, it's important to know how to observe the rules of each category of airspace before you try flying through (or near) them. Furthermore, obeying the rules takes an active approach, because the boundaries are all arbitrarily drawn on a map—you won't see a fence sectioning off these areas, so you'll have to know where they are on your own.

Two sets of rules govern all air traffic. One set is called Visual Flight Rules (VFR), and the other is known as Instrument Flight Rules (IFR). For each of the different classifications of airspace, there are minimum permissible weather conditions required for safe visual flight. Any weather conditions better (that is to say, clearer) than these minimums permit pilots to fly under VFR.

When meteorological conditions fall below those required for VFR flight, Instrument Meteorological Conditions (IMC) prevail. When flying in IMC and any time flying at 18,000 feet and above, IFR rules apply. Often during IMC, maintaining visual separation (and, of course, visual navigation) is difficult if not impossible, so air traffic control is responsible for keeping all aircraft separated.

N O T A M

Notice to All Airmen

In good weather, both VFR and IFR aircraft operate under the principle of visual separation, in which all pilots are responsible for noticing (and avoiding!) other aircraft, regardless of their flight plans.

In order to give air traffic control (ATC) the authority it needs to accomplish this, the sky is divided into various classes of airspace. The definitions and names of the airspace classes in the United States are based upon international conventions and correspond to letters of the alphabet. The later the letter in the alphabet, the looser the restrictions on aircraft in that airspace type.

Airspace classes are divided into two broad categories: controlled and uncontrolled. Class G airspace is the only type of uncontrolled airspace in the U.S., with all other classes (A through E) falling into the controlled airspace category.

Uncontrolled Airspace

Air traffic control has no authority or responsibility for controlling aircraft in Class G airspace, regardless of the weather. As such, you may fly in Class G airspace without contacting ATC. In Visual Meterological Conditions (VMC), even aircraft flying under IFR by using control and a filed flight plan must still remain alert and avoid VFR traffic. In IMC, the opposite applies—all aircraft *must* have clearance from ATC to fly, and all airspace is considered controlled. VFR flight is prohibited by weather that is below the category minimums. To fly in these conditions, both the aircraft *and* the pilot must be certified for IFR flight.

Class G airspace is divided into three layers, based upon altitude above ground level (AGL). During daylight hours, the regulations for VFR flight in these layers are as follows:

ALTITUDE	MINIMUM VISIBILITY	MINIMUM DISTANCE FROM CLOUDS
<1,200' AGL	1 mile	Remain clear
1,200' AGL–10,000' MSL	1 mile	>500' below
		>1,000' above
		>1 mile horizontally
>10,000' MSL	5 miles	>1,000' below
		>1,000' above
		>1 mile horizontally

At night, these minimums change somewhat:

ALTITUDE	MINIMUM VISIBILITY	MINIMUM DISTANCE FROM CLOUDS
<1,200' AGL	3 miles	>500' below
		>1,000' above
		>2,000' horizontally
1,200' AGL–10,000' MSL	3 miles	>500' below
		>1,000' above
		>1 mile horizontally
>10,000' MSL	5 miles	>1,000' below
		>1,000' above
		>1 mile horizontally

Note that an aircraft in the traffic pattern within one-half mile of the runway may always operate in conditions of at least one-mile visibility and simply remain clear of clouds.

Controlled Airspace

In general, controlled airspace has only two divisions, separated by an arbitrary boundary at 10,000 feet MSL (Mean Sea Level). Each division has its own set of restrictions designed to promote safe flight.

ALTITUDE	MINIMUM VISIBILITY	MINIMUM DISTANCE FROM CLOUDS
<10,000' MSL	3 miles	>500' below
		>1,000' above
		>2,000' horizontally
>10,000' MSL	5 miles	>1,000' below
		>1,000' above
		>1 mile horizontally

Note that "controlled airspace" is a bit of a misnomer—you're not *always* required to communicate with ATC and/or operate on a clearance; it's airspace over which an authority can exercise control and within which pilots must adhere to certain rules, including compliance with ATC directions. Often those rules include communicating with ATC, but not always. Aircraft may still fly freely under VFR so long as they maintain visual separation from other aircraft and clouds. In addition, IFR services are available to qualified instrument-rated pilots within controlled airspace. Each class of controlled airspace has a different standard altitude, shape, and regulations governing passage through it. Figure 3.2 shows

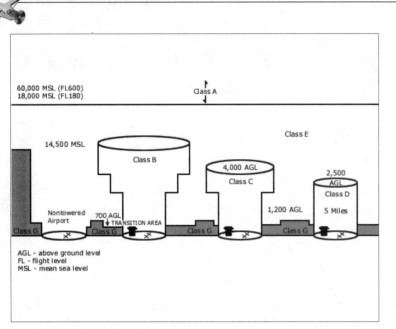

Figure 3.2 *U.S. airspace classifications*

the various airspace classifications in use in the United States. Note that they are generally based around an airport or an airway.

The following sections describe the classes of controlled airspace from least to most controlled (E through A). Note that Class F airspace does not apply in the U.S.

Class E Airspace

Class E airspace comes in two flavors: ground-based and elevated (see Figure 3.3). Ground-based Class E airspace is found around airports that do not have an active control tower but do offer official weather observations and an instrument approach system. Note that if there are ever times at which no weather service is available, the area is downgraded to Class G airspace.

The primary purpose of ground-based Class E airspace is to give IFR pilots landing at the airport a buffer zone from VFR traffic. Ground-based Class E airspace is denoted on VFR charts by a magenta dashed line around the airport symbol and often includes an approach corridor. The airspace extends vertically to the base of whatever airspace overlays it. This often forms the base of elevated Class E airspace.

Elevated Class E airspace has three standard base altitudes: 700 feet AGL, 1,200 feet AGL, or 14,500 feet MSL. A shaded magenta border fading into the interior of a zone denotes a 700-foot base. If the border is colored blue instead, the Class E airspace begins at 1,400 feet AGL. If the Class E airspace starts at any other (nonstandard) altitude, it will be marked with a black "tire tread" zigzag line, with the altitude printed beside it.

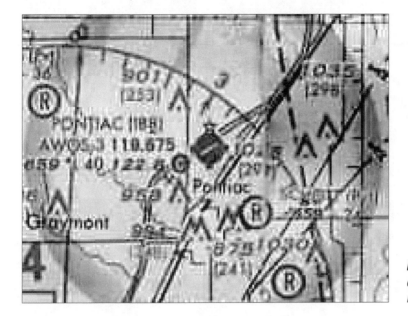

Figure 3.3 *Ground-based and elevated Class E airspace chart notations*

You need clearance to operate within Class E airspace only when the weather is below minimum VFR limits. At all other times, clearance from or contact with ATC may not be required, so you should fly standard airport traffic patterns (described in Chapter 5: Creating a Flight Plan) and use the Common Traffic Advisory Frequency (CTAF) to monitor traffic and announce your intentions.

Class D Airspace

Surface-based, controlled Class D airspace surrounds airports with operating control towers. You'll find it marked on a chart with a blue dashed line around an airport. As a rule of thumb, they are generally five statute miles in radius, although each boundary is tailored to the associated airport with one or more rectangular extensions to keep VFR traffic clear of aircraft on Instrument Landing System (ILS) approaches (as shown in Figure 3.4). If the tower shuts down (as many do at night), the airspace is downgraded to Class E. If no weather service is available during this time, it is further downgraded to Class G.

Operations within Class D airspace require two-way communication with the airport's control tower. Usually, Class D airspace extends to 2,500 feet above the airport elevation. The upper limit is shown on charts as a number enclosed in a dashed line box (see Figure 3.4), expressed in hundreds-of-feet MSL. Even if you are landing at an uncontrolled airport nearby, you must contact the tower controlling the airspace if your approach path or the destination runway falls within the Class D airspace. Also, you should contact the tower as soon as possible when departing this kind of outlying field.

Figure 3.4 *Class D airspace is denoted by a blue dashed line.*

You may on occasion see Class D airspace with a "bite" out of it to specifically exclude a satellite airport; in such a case, be advised that the Class D airspace usually extends over the top of the exclusion zone, usually starting at 1,200 feet AGL.

Class C Airspace

Class C airspace looks like a little bit like a mushroom, with a small cylinder at ground level and a larger one sitting on top of it (see Figure 3.5). The inner cylinder has a standard radius of five nautical miles and usually extends from ground level to 1,200 feet AGL. The outer ring has a 10-mile radius, and it extends from the top of the first ring to an altitude of 4,000 feet above the airport elevation. On an aeronautical chart, you'll see a set of numbers in each ring. The number above the line shows the upper altitude limit of the ring, in hundreds-of-feet MSL. The lower number shows the base of the airspace, with "SFC" representing the ground surface.

Radar Control

Class C airspace and all remaining classes use radar services to help manage traffic. However, the primary responsibility for collision avoidance remains with the pilot in command—and that's you. Aircraft under radar guidance are directed with vectors, which prescribe a heading and sometimes an altitude and airspeed. Even when operating on an assigned vector, you must constantly monitor your own position and those of the aircraft around you, and even refuse to comply if a given instruction will put your aircraft or others in peril.

Figure 3.5 *Class C airspace looks like two concentric circles with a solid magenta border.*

An outer area is associated with all Class C airspace that is not recorded on charts. This ring reaches out to a 20-mile radius around the airport, though its exact dimensions may vary based upon local requirements. The base of the outer area is generally at the surface, though areas with rugged terrain may be unable to offer radar coverage at lower altitudes. The upper limit of the outer area is defined by the ceiling of the approach control's designated airspace.

Radio communication with air traffic control is required prior to entering or departing Class C airspace. Contact with control must also be maintained while operating within Class C boundaries. Aircraft that depart nearby airports are required to establish communication with the tower as soon as possible. While you are in Class C airspace, ATC will provide the following services:

➤ Orderly landing queuing of all aircraft on approach

➤ Traffic advisories and collision avoidance between IFR and VFR traffic

➤ VFR traffic advisories to help VFR pilots spot each other and maintain safe separation

These services are continued in the outer service area so long as two-way communication and radar contact can be maintained. In the outer area, however, you are not required to contact ATC. As such, a pilot may request the discontinuation of service while in this area. ATC may provide radar service even beyond the outer area, but only if the controller has the time.

Class B Airspace

This class of airspace is for the busiest of airports. Its heavy restrictions exist to help slot arriving and departing aircraft into proper sequences, and to facilitate safe separation distances in the dense traffic. Class B airspace extends for several miles around the airport, with ceilings and floors that are tailored to the airport's traffic flows and to accommodate local geography, adjacent airspace, and so forth. These dimensions are expressed with solid blue borders on aeronautical charts, as shown in Figure 3.6. They use the same over/under method to show the base and ceiling altitudes of each section.

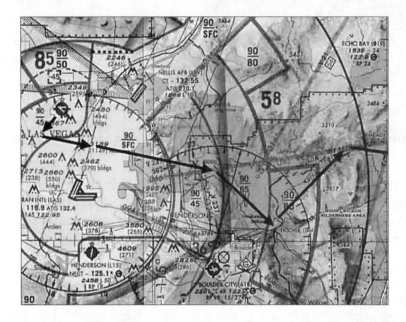

Figure 3.6 Class B airspace is unmistakable on a chart, with its complex blue zones.

All pilots flying into or out of Class B airspace must establish radio contact with TRACON (Terminal Radar Approach Control Facility) and hear the magic words, "Cleared to enter the Class B airspace," before proceeding. Because of the heavy air traffic in these areas, all aircraft must submit to radar service. VFR traffic has to remain clear of clouds, but normal separation limits do not apply; VFR pilots are free to approach clouds so long as they remain outside of them. VFR pilots are required to operate with a transponder while in Class B airspace.

Class A Airspace

All VFR airspace has a ceiling of 17,999 feet MSL in North America. Above this altitude, Class A airspace extends to 60,000 feet MSL. All pilots and planes entering Class A airspace must be IFR qualified and must have an IFR clearance from air traffic control. Beginning at 18,000 feet MSL, all pilots reset their altimeters to 29.92 instead of their local settings, which ensures that everyone flying in Class A airspace is using the same basis for measurement. Setting all altimeters to 29.92 guarantees that 25,000 feet means the same altitude to everyone, regardless of where their flight originated.

Because all altimeters use the standardized pressure setting of 29.92, altitudes in Class A airspace have a special name or designation: "flight level." A flight level expresses altitude in hundreds of feet, meaning a pressure altitude of 30,000 feet is flight level 300.

Special-Use Airspace

Other kinds of airspace out there are generally off-limits. Military testing ranges, top-secret installations (Groom Lake, anyone?), and other types of restricted airspace either restrict or pose a threat to transient air traffic. As such, it's usually best to find a way around these areas. However, some do not require clearance to enter, so the following information will help you decide where you want (and don't want) to go.

Military Operations Areas (MOAs)

You'll find these zones listed on charts with a magenta border that has hash lines running across it, like a zipper. They are always named with the letters "MOA" inside. These areas are used by the military for high-speed flights, high-volume traffic, special training missions, or other such operations unfriendly to civilian light aircraft.

Alert Areas

These zones are areas in which the military has heavy training, dense air traffic, or other activities in the region. These areas are shown by a blue "zippered" border similar to that around regular MOAs. Special permission is not required to enter Alert Areas, but pilots should be especially attentive when flying in them. They are defined by a zone on a sectional chart marked with the letter "A" followed by the alert area's number.

Military Training Routes

These corridors are used for special low-altitude, high-speed flights by the military. Such routes are designated with gray lines on an aeronautical chart. Altitude information is discerned by the numbering. An IR (instrument route) or VR (visual route) with a four-digit number is at or below 1,500 feet AGL. Routes that may extend up to 10,000 feet MSL are designated by a three-digit code. These routes are not restricted, but civil aircraft should avoid flying within them; if you have to, fly parallel to the route with a two-mile separation.

Prohibited Areas

Prohibited areas are absolutely off-limits to all aircraft without specific government clearance. This classification is used sparingly in the United States, but it includes all areas where overflight by aircraft would be a risk to national security. No unauthorized aircraft are

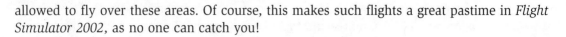

allowed to fly over these areas. Of course, this makes such flights a great pastime in *Flight Simulator 2002*, as no one can catch you!

Restricted Areas

Weapon test ranges and military training areas (different from Military Training Routes) are usually classified as restricted airspace. They may be flown over with specific permission from the controlling agency (which you can simply assume in *Flight Simulator 2002*) or sometimes by observance of specific time restrictions, which will be noted on the sectional chart. Restricted areas are usually described in a table entry on the outside of a chart for reference, including contact information for the controlling authority. It is vital for aircraft to observe the restrictions, lest they become the inadvertent victims of a weapons test.

Altitudes

Now that you know where to fly, it's time to take a look at how high to fly there. VFR traffic flying at or above 3,000 feet is organized around a general rule: NEOdd, SWEven (north and east, odd; south and west, even). VFR traffic on a northern or eastern course (headings from 360 to 179 degrees clockwise) should use odd-numbered altitudes (measured in thousands of feet) plus 500 feet, while VFR traffic on southern or western courses (headings from 180 to 359 degrees clockwise) should use even-numbered altitudes plus 500 feet. IFR traffic uses the same NEOdd and SWEven rule, but without the additional 500 feet. This provides a 500-foot cushion between VFR and IFR traffic flying in the same direction. Figure 3.7 shows the standard cruising altitudes for air traffic. You can select any of the prescribed altitudes so long as

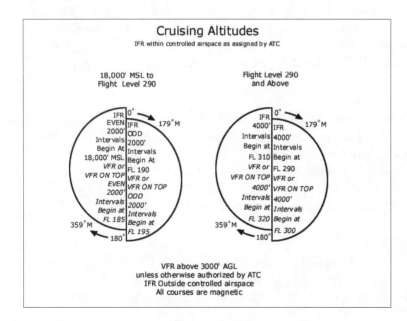

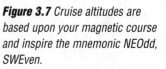

Figure 3.7 *Cruise altitudes are based upon your magnetic course and inspire the mnemonic NEOdd, SWEven.*

you comply with the minimum established for the route and your aircraft is capable of reliably achieving your selected altitude.

VFR Navigation

Now that you know the rules of the "roads" you'll be traveling, it's time to learn how to find your way around. Once again, there are no road signs or roadways in the air (at least none that you can see). This means you can't just start a trip by pointing your nose in the right direction, the way you can with an automobile. Without some way to keep track of where you are and where you are going, you can easily get completely lost.

> **N O T A M**
> **Notice to All Airmen**
>
> VFR flight has its advantages and disadvantages. Although it's enjoyable to have the freedom of movement afforded by a nonspecific flight plan as a recreational pilot, VFR is permitted only when the weather conditions are clear enough to support visual separation and navigation. VFR pilots are grounded when the visibility and/or ceiling drops.

The most straightforward method of aerial navigation is under Visual Flight Rules (VFR). As described previously, VFR traffic is the most loosely regulated type of traffic and operates with the greatest amount of freedom—you are generally free to fly in any direction you wish, and even in most controlled airspace, you do not have to declare a specific destination (see Figure 3.8). As described in the Getting More file in the *Flight Simulator 2002* on-disc documentation, the first flight certification achieved is a VFR Private Pilot rating. As such, we'll examine visual navigation methods first.

Figure 3.8 *VFR flight plans give you the freedom to chase down rainbows (or whatever else suits your fancy).*

Visual Navigation Methods

In practice, pilots usually employ a combination of every method of navigation available to them in a modern aircraft: landmarks, course and speed estimation, radio equipment, radar control instructions, and even Global Positioning System (GPS) data. This practical application of all information available is called composite navigation, and it's what 99% of pilots do every day. For the sake of clarity, this section deals exclusively with non-electronic methods of navigation.

Pilots in the early era of flight navigated with diligent map work, a little math computation, some landmark following, and a bit of luck. With some training, you'll be able to put away the modern electronics and figure out where you're going all on your own. The two primary methods of unaided aerial navigation are pilotage and dead reckoning, both of which are described below.

Pilotage

Pilotage is navigation by visible landmarks. It represents the simplest method of finding the way to your destination. Essentially, you fly from one known landmark to the next by visual reference and known compass headings. All you need to navigate by pilotage is clear visibility, a sectional VFR chart like the one in Figure 3.9, a straightedge for drawing lines, a compass, and a clock to make sure you're arriving at checkpoints on time and won't run out of fuel.

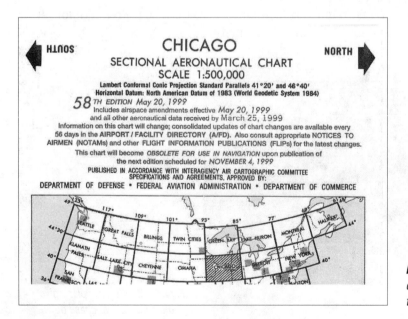

Figure 3.9 *Sectional charts provide detailed map information of interest to aviators.*

Obviously, pilotage is possible only if you can see the ground. As such, it is fundamentally tied to VFR conditions. To navigate to your destination, you must determine your position (sometimes called getting a fix) by looking at surrounding landmarks and then picking the next landmark to fly to. Since it would be difficult to pick landmarks in the middle of your flight, the following preflight steps are required:

1. Begin by obtaining the proper sectional chart and identifying your origin and destination.

2. Determine the general character of the route between the two airports, or the area over which you wish to fly in the case of a roundtrip. Make special note of any restricted areas, high peaks, or other points you'd like to avoid flying over.

3. Determine a course line, selecting landmarks that lie as close as possible to the centerline of your desired track.

4. Measure the total distance of your flight plan by comparing the total length of all flight legs with the map scale. You must be sure that your plane has adequate fuel for the trip, as well as a healthy reserve in case your flight is unexpectedly extended due to navigation or landing troubles, headwinds, or any number of other possible complications.

5. Select checkpoints along the route that will serve as specific landmarks to help you track your progress and obtain position fixes in flight. At each landmark, you can adjust your heading to intersect the next checkpoint properly. It is important to update your heading each time you find a landmark, as errors have a tendency to compound themselves and you will risk getting lost.

The key to good pilotage is selecting good checkpoints. Immovable, permanent objects such as distinctive buildings, rivers, roads, towns, mountain peaks, towers, and so on are good choices. A nondescript warehouse, a barn in the Great Plains, a parked RV, or something else that is either impermanent or easily mistaken is not a good choice, nor is something that is wonderfully unique but too small to be seen from the air. An ideal landmark is one that not only identifies your position, but also the direction in which you're facing. Section lines, the sun, and orientation of highways and bodies of water are great indicators of your direction—along with your compass, of course.

Another good idea is to designate landmark pairs that bracket your intended course. That way you have a larger margin for error if you stray from your track. For example, if you intend to pass over a checkpoint with a coal mine on your left and a small town on your right, but then find yourself on the proper heading but with the coal mine on your right, you know you've missed the small town com-

N O T A M
Notice to All Airmen

Pilotage is ideal for clear-day flying over familiar terrain, short hops, or trips up a continuous feature like a river or highway.

pletely. Quick deduction reveals that the town is probably farther off to your right, beyond the coal mine. If you had chosen the small town as a single landmark, you may have missed it entirely.

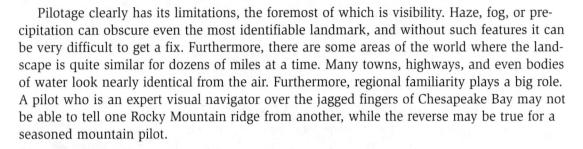

Pilotage clearly has its limitations, the foremost of which is visibility. Haze, fog, or precipitation can obscure even the most identifiable landmark, and without such features it can be very difficult to get a fix. Furthermore, there are some areas of the world where the landscape is quite similar for dozens of miles at a time. Many towns, highways, and even bodies of water look nearly identical from the air. Furthermore, regional familiarity plays a big role. A pilot who is an expert visual navigator over the jagged fingers of Chesapeake Bay may not be able to tell one Rocky Mountain ridge from another, while the reverse may be true for a seasoned mountain pilot.

Dead Reckoning

Dead reckoning (DR), sometimes referred to as ded reckoning since it is short for "deduced reckoning," is actually a more scientific approach to navigation than pilotage. DR remains the oldest method of navigation still in use, though most pilots currently employ a combination of pilotage and electronic navigation. The general idea is to fly your plane on a direct path to your destination by maintaining a set compass heading that accurately compensates for all the effects that alter your ground track. Compass variations, the difference between magnetic north and true north, and even regional magnetic differences increase the difference between a magnetic compass reading from your true course, but none of these has a greater potential for inducing variation than wind, and it's the hardest to estimate. But if you can precisely factor in all these elements, you can calculate your precise position by comparing time elapsed, true ground speed, and actual course. Relieved of the need to look for specific landmarks, you can fly longer routes over unknown terrain and use direct flightpaths instead of adjusting your track to intercept checkpoints.

Although it requires some complex calculations, DR is an extremely useful skill. Most pilots (and even automobile drivers) use it in some form, if only subconsciously. For example, when considering a lengthy trip, most drivers consider their anticipated average speed and arrive at an estimated trip time based upon that speed over the given distance. Experienced drivers go a step further and plan for any anticipated slowdowns, such as rush hour traffic and road construction. DR is just like that! There are merely a few additional factors to consider in a plane: wind speed, magnetic variation, compass deviation…OK, so it's a little more complicated than driving (see Figure 3.10).

In order to use DR, you have to compare your airplane's heading and indicated airspeed with its ground track and ground speed. The procedure outlined below will help you figure it out without too much trouble.

Course Plotting The first step in DR navigation is figuring out what course you want to fly. Take a straightedge and draw a line between your point of origin and your destination on a sectional chart. If you don't have an aeronautical plotter, you can use a straightedge and protractor to measure your designated course; the line on the chart is the track you want to fly. You can also use *Flight Simulator 2002*'s Flight Planner to auto-generate the course for

Figure 3.10 *Crosswinds can be especially troublesome for DR navigation.*

you. Simply select the origin and destination airports, and have the Flight Planner "find a route" for you via direct (GPS) vectors. Your flight plan will then show the required course, as seen in Figure 3.11.

Wind Effect Now that you know the course to fly, you must determine what heading takes you in that direction and how fast you will travel while on it. If there is a crosswind, you

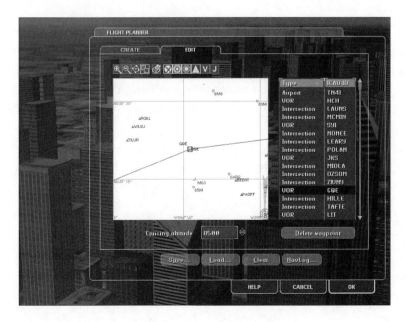

Figure 3.11 *The Flight Planner can be used to determine your desired course.*

won't actually go in the direction your nose is pointing, because the air constantly pushes you in another direction. If there is a headwind or tailwind, you go over the ground slower or faster (respectively) than your airspeed indicator suggests.

A combination of two factors is involved in aircraft movement: its motion through the air and the motion of the air over the ground. By using a wind triangle that combines these two effects, you can calculate where your plane is going. Your objective, of course, is to fly your plane along the course line you drew on the chart (or along the course you calculated using the Flight Planner). To correct for a crosswind, angle the nose into the wind just enough to offset the drift caused by the crosswind. This angle is called the wind correction angle, or WCA. To figure out the WCA, you have to know these things: wind speed, wind direction, the airplane's true airspeed, and your true or magnetic course, depending on whether you use winds referenced to true or magnetic north. *Flight Simulator 2002* will tell you the first two pieces of information in its Weather menu screen.

If your trip isn't going to be an hour in length, divide both your true airspeed and the wind speed in half in order to plot a shorter distance on your chart when drawing a wind triangle. Just remember that you're plotting only a half-hour's worth of travel instead of the usual hour.

True Airspeed To figure out your true airspeed, either calculate it yourself or set the airspeed indicator to display true airspeed instead of indicated airspeed. Calculating it yourself is significantly more difficult and involves math work that is beyond the scope of this guide. If you're willing to give it a go, you must calculate the absolute tailwind or headwind component of the prevailing winds at your flight altitude, and add or subtract that total from your indicated airspeed.

WCA Plotting When you know your true airspeed, measure out an hour's worth of travel at your desired flight speed on your ground track. If you intend to maintain a speed of 120 knots over your trip, measure 120 nautical miles. Next, draw the wind line from the origin, in the direction that the wind is blowing. Measure a number of nautical miles equal to the wind speed in knots along the wind line and plot that distance as the wind point. You've now plotted two points: your position in an hour without any wind and the motion of the wind over that hour.

Now, draw the third side of the triangle, connecting your wind point to the ground track plot point. This third line points in the direction of the heading you need to fly on in order to travel along your plotted course. Figure 3.12 shows a completed WCA plot for a 30-knot wind blowing at 60 degrees across the intended direction of travel.

Obviously, DR navigation is somewhat cumbersome and subject to error. Not only are the calculations easy to botch, but the method assumes a constant wind speed. When dealing with gusting winds or changing weather, your mileage may vary (literally). As such, DR is best used in combination with pilotage, or better yet, more modern forms of navigation. The following section introduces you to those new ways to get from point A to point B.

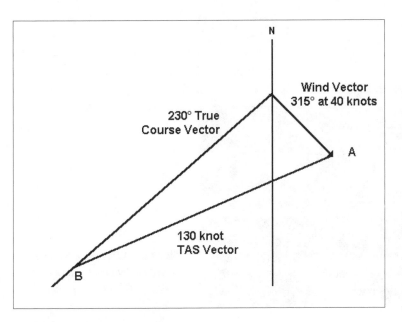

Figure 3.12 labels: N, Wind Vector 315° at 40 knots, 230° True Course Vector, A, 130 knot TAS Vector, B

Figure 3.12 *Plotting the WCA is a somewhat complicated business, but it can help you avoid checkpoints.*

IFR Navigation

Advances in technology have made aerial navigation much easier since the early days, primarily through the application of radio signals. A wide variety of radio-based systems is the principal means of long-distance navigation for aircraft today. Those systems form the basis of IFR flight. In this section, we'll examine the various methods of radio navigation and show you how to apply them to your own navigational needs.

The Ground School document in your *Flight Simulator 2002* online manual contains exhaustive information on VHF Omnidirectional Ranges (VORs) and ILS navigation. Rather than repeat that material here, we'll cover the essentials for use as a reference. Check out Lessons 11, 16, and 17 of Ground School before digging into the material below. We'll also take a look at the IFR training panel models to help you use them as valuable piloting tools.

VOR Navigation

VORs use very high frequency (VHF) radio transmissions to transmit a signal in all directions (omnidirectional). The VOR transmits a series of 360 signals, or radials, rotating around a circle in one-degree increments. Radials are identified by numbers beginning with 001 (one degree east of magnetic north) and continue through all the degrees of a circle until reaching 360. Aircraft that intercept these radials can determine their position from the beacon (see Figure 3.13).

Figure 3.13 This plane has intersected the 90-degree radial of the selected VOR, meaning it is due east of the station.

VORs are the most commonly used navigational aids (navaids for short) in aviation. Pilots can tune in a specific bearing beam (radial) from a specific station and use it to fly directly to or from the station. They can also use it in conjunction with a second station to navigate to specific waypoints in the air at virtually any desired location. Both methods of navigation are thoroughly described in the Ground School online manual. Here, you'll learn how to apply those procedures to practical navigation.

Distance Measuring Equipment

Many VORs today have associated Distance Measuring Equipment (DME) so that you can get not only the bearing from the station, but also the straight-line distance between the station and the aircraft. You just tune a VOR with DME, determine your radial, and read the distance from the station—there, you've got a fix.

A typical DME indicator

It's important to remember that DME measures "slant-range distance," the direct distance from the plane to the DME ground facility, so it's accounting for altitude. Therefore, if you are flying directly over the VOR at 6,000 feet (the equivalent of one nautical mile), your DME will read one mile. At 18,000 feet directly over the VOR, your DME will indicate three miles. This effect is negligible when you are over 10 miles from the station, but you should bear your altitude in mind when operating at closer ranges.

Proceeding Direct

The easiest way to use a VOR station is to tune its frequency on your NAV radio, adjust the OBS (Omni Bearing Selector) until the To-From indicator displays "TO," and then continue turning the OBS until the course deviation indicator (CDI) is centered. Once you've got the CDI needle in the right place, read your designated OBS course. This is the course you must fly in order to head directly toward the station. Note that your required heading may not be exactly the same. If you are in a crosswind, you'll have to correct by angling your nose into the wind somewhat (see Figure 3.14).

Figure 3.14 *This plane is in a heavy crosswind flying a steady course toward the VOR station.*

If you drift off the needle when your heading is matched with the radial selected, swing your nose up to 25–30 degrees in the direction of the needle. When it centers again, begin moving back to your original heading, but stay five degrees short of it. If you fall off again, repeat the procedure and increase the difference between your heading and the OBS course. Eventually, you'll find a heading that will keep you centered on the radial, which will mean that you've successfully corrected for the crosswind.

Two-Station Fixes

If the VOR station includes DME, you can determine how far you are from the station. A quick look at a chart tells you exactly where you are. Simply measure the indicated

TIP

Use VOR intersections to provide ongoing updates of your position. Simply leave your NAV radio tuned to the second VOR and periodically adjust the OBS to keep the needle centered as you move past the radials.

distance from the station to which you are tuned along the bearing corresponding to the radial you've dialed in on the OBS. Without DME, you can still obtain a precise fix by using two VOR stations.

To obtain a two-station fix, proceed directly to or from one VOR along any radial. After you are established on this radial, tune a second VOR that lies to either side of your course (one that is located perpendicular to your course to the first VOR is ideal, though this will not always be easily determined). Make sure you've got a FROM indication to avoid selecting the reciprocal course from the second VOR. Adjust the OBS until you center the needle (with a FROM indication) and make a note of the indicated radial. Draw a line from the first station along your first radial, and then draw a line from the second station along the second radial. Don't be alarmed if the two lines don't intersect—you've probably just tuned to the reciprocal heading of the second station. If this happens, plot its line in the opposite direction to intercept your first radial.

The point at which the lines cross is your current position. If your angular velocity (the rate at which you're moving across the radials) relative to the second station is high, you can simply note when you cross a given radial to obtain a fix (see Figure 3.15).

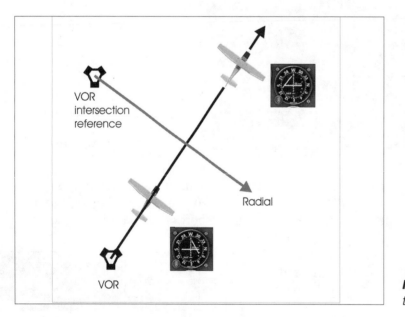

Figure 3.15 Watch the CDI closely to obtain a precise fix.

You can also use two VORs to obtain a fix even if you are not heading directly to or from either of the stations. Start by tuning the first station and adjusting the OBS until the CDI needle is centered. Make sure that the To-From indicator shows "FROM," as that is the useful bearing *from* the station. Take note of this first radial, and then quickly tune to a second VOR and repeat the process. You will soon have an intersecting pair of lines that mark your location with reasonable accuracy, but they won't represent your exact position because by the time you draw the lines, you've flown past the position designated by the intersection of the radial. Because VOR radials spread out like light beams, as you get farther away from the station, the beam increases and your measurements aren't as precise.

Two things will help minimize this error. First, take your measurements as close together as possible. Second, use VOR stations that are farther away from you to minimize your angular velocity; an intermediate distance of 20–30 miles generally works for all aircraft except jets. An aircraft going 120 knots at a 30-mile distance from a given VOR crosses each radial much more slowly than an aircraft going the same speed at a distance of one mile. To imagine this, picture yourself standing next to a runway when a plane takes off. You have to move your head from one side to the other very quickly to keep the aircraft in view. Conversely, watching a plane in flight several miles away barely requires any head movement at all, even though it is probably going much faster than the vehicle that is just lifting off.

IFR Training Panels

Flight Simulator 2002 Professional Edition *includes special expanded instrument panels on several of the aircraft. These panels take up most of the screen and keep all of your IFR instrumentation in view at all times. This is the perfect way to work on your IFR flying skills, since you'll have very little view out of the cockpit. In IMC (instrument meteorological conditions), there isn't much to see out there anyway, so the IFR training panels are a great aid to navigation and piloting.*

Note that you can still see out while maintaining an eye on your instrumentation by pressing the "W" key once. This will bring up a view over the nose of your plane, but you'll still see your primary flight instruments. This is a new and welcome feature in Flight Simulator 2002. *With it, you can enjoy the scenery without the instrument panel, while still keeping your plane under precise control. To bring the full instrument panel back up, cycle through the cockpit views two more times.*

Non-Directional Beacons

Non-directional beacons (NDBs) are halfway between DMEs and VORs. You can easily figure out your bearing from the station by tuning your automatic direction finder (ADF) to the NDB. The ADF's arrowhead points in the direction you need to fly to reach the NDB station, and the tail points in the direction your aircraft is located relative to the NDB. It's a little harder to track to or from an NDB station than a VOR station because the relative bearing to the station changes whenever the aircraft's heading changes while orientation with a VOR is independent of the aircraft's heading, resulting in a more steady, easy-to-follow course.

The easiest way to use an NDB is to treat it like a homing beacon. Since the ADF arrow will point toward the NDB station, you can mentally superimpose the arrow over your heading indicator (HI) to quickly determine the proper magnetic heading to intercept the station (see Figure 3.16). Adjusting your heading to the arrowhead will then take you directly to the station, while flying toward the tail will take you directly away from it. Strong winds aloft will play games with you while attempting to fly direct to the station. Without establishing the necessary wind correction heading (a truly acquired art!), you may wind up flying a more curved route to the station, but you will get there.

Figure 3.16 Mentally superimpose the ADF needle on the HI to find the magnetic bearing to the station.

CHAPTER 4
Spreading Your Wings

This chapter will teach you advanced flight maneuvers and concepts, as well as emergency procedures. Note that advanced maneuvers aren't necessarily optional maneuvers—many are essential tools for the well-rounded pilot. While you might not put your Skyhawk through a barrel roll on every flight, being familiar with it (albeit in a more suitable aircraft, such as the Extra 300S) will give you the ability to respond to unforeseen in-flight situations with speed and competence. Familiarity with emergency procedures is also very useful, as Flight Simulator 2002 provides you with the opportunity to put your emergency piloting skills to use!

Emergencies

Flight Simulator 2002 allows pilots to experience an enormous range of in-flight emergencies. These break down into four causes, as follows:

➤ Programmed failures

➤ Random failures

➤ Instructor's Station-induced failures

➤ Pilot error

Each of the above can induce one or more of three general categories of emergency, listed below:

➤ Instrument failures

➤ Mechanical failures

➤ Departures from controlled flight

This section describes in-flight emergencies—creating them, avoiding them, and most importantly of all, recovering from them.

Creating Emergencies

In-flight emergencies can greatly enhance your enjoyment of the simulation when you're looking for a challenge. Alternatively, you're able to ensure a perfectly reliable aircraft if the idea of falling out of the simulated sky (see Figure 4.1) isn't your cup of tea (you can even

Figure 4.1 *This chapter will help you keep in-flight emergencies in flight.*

get around pilot error by turning crashes off). *Flight Simulator 2002* provides you with a robust suite of options for introducing failures into your flight for an added challenge.

To set up system and instrument failures, go to the Aircraft menu and click System Failures. You have two basic choices in the System Failures menu: programmed failures or random failures. Together, they offer an excellent range of control over the types of emergencies that you'll experience in the air.

Programmed Failures

Programmed failures are set up by selecting a specific aircraft system and establishing a time range in which that system will fail, measured from the time that you enter the simulation. You can "bracket" a particular moment in your flight so that the failure happens exactly when you expect it to, or you can introduce an element of surprise by widening the specified time frame. If you want to ensure that a failure never occurs, clear the check boxes. If you want to make the probability of a failure occurring low, enter a long time frame.

TIP

It's best to specify a minimum programmed failure time of at least five minutes, or however long you think it will take you to roll for takeoff. Mechanical malfunction on the ramp is an automatic reason to cancel a flight, so for greater realism, try to time the failure so that it doesn't happen until after your rotation on takeoff.

The advantage of using programmed failures is that you can specify exactly which system you'd like to fail. This can be useful if you're trying to practice a specific kind of emergency. In addition, if you aren't a whiz with failure diagnosis, this method greatly simplifies your response. So when your altimeter goes, you won't have to puzzle over whether the gauge is malfunctioning, your electrical system is down, your pitot static system is failing, or a goose is protruding from your pitot tube.

Random Failures

You can also enable random failures in the System Failures dialog box. These failures can affect any system in the aircraft at any time, and you can specify the likelihood of a failure occurring. Set the reliability factor low enough, and you're likely to have several failures in a single flight. Set it very high, and you might encounter a failure only once over the course of several flights.

TIP

You can set up a mix of random and programmed failures by using multiple programmed failures. Select a very long maximum time for the failure of several systems, and you may experience the failure of one, some, or all of the selected systems during your flight. If you want fewer failures (and the potential for none at all), set a longer maximum time.

Random failures present you with an added level of challenge because you'll have to notice the failure and then diagnose the problem. Unlike programmed failures, you can't simply keep an eye on the gauge(s) or system(s) selected for failure; random failures force you to watch everything. Of course, this added challenge comes at the cost of simplicity. In an aircraft, each component is tied to many others through complex interactions. If you aren't familiar with the way these systems work together, you may have trouble determining the exact failure that has befallen your aircraft, leading to additional complications.

Instructor's Station-Induced Failures

Flight Simulator 2002 Professional Edition includes a special multiplayer mode that re-creates an option previously found only in flight training simulators that cost tens of thousands of dollars. This mode allows another user, called the instructor, to create system failures in your aircraft. The instructor has the power to induce a wide range of malfunctions in your aircraft, ranging from faulty indicators to engine failure. This is an ideal training aid (unless your instructor is overly sadistic) because the instructor can control all events in a thoughtful, meaningful manner. Setting up an Instructor Station session is thoroughly explained in the Training Features online handbook that shipped with your copy of the simulation and is also expanded upon in Chapter 9: Sharing the Sky.

Pilot Error

Pilot error can cause a wide range of failures and emergencies. The leading causes of serious accidents are loss of control during low-altitude maneuvering and flying into marginal weather. One of the most fundamental mistakes is losing control of the aircraft through a "departure from controlled flight," commonly just called a "departure," a term that describes any loss of control as a result of pushing the aircraft outside of its safe flight envelope.

Not all pilot errors are related to departures, however. Accidentally turning systems off, improper equipment settings, center of gravity errors, inadequate fuel supply, and a host of other issues can get pilots into unnecessary emergencies. You may encounter any one of these kinds of errors in the realistic world of *Flight Simulator 2002*, whether it be through improperly calculating your fuel supply, departure from controlled flight, or hitting the wrong key and accidentally shutting down or adjusting a system.

Emergency Procedures

As mentioned above, there are three general categories of in-flight emergencies. System failures affect one or more of your instruments or aircraft systems and can be fairly minor, while mechanical failures can be more serious and may even limit your ability to control the aircraft. As there are many types of pilot error, the following section focuses solely on recovering from departures. The paragraphs below address each kind of emergency and arm you with the tools needed to work through them.

Instrument Failures

Unless you're operating in Instrument Meterological Conditions (IMC), instrument failures are among the least severe emergencies you can experience during a flight. Although the loss of an instrument is inconvenient, most modern aircraft have several redundant gauges and systems that allow you to find most of the malfunctioning instrument's information in other places. Read on for more advice on how to cope with individual instrument failures.

Airspeed Indicator Your airspeed indicator is one of the only instruments that doesn't have a directly redundant reading on other displays. You can, however, still use your GPS (Global Positioning System) to estimate your airspeed. The GPS shows ground speed (GS), but unless you're flying with a strong headwind or tailwind, GS is close to airspeed (see Figure 4.2). You can also estimate your airspeed by looking out the window and noting the time required to travel between two points when the distance between the points is known.

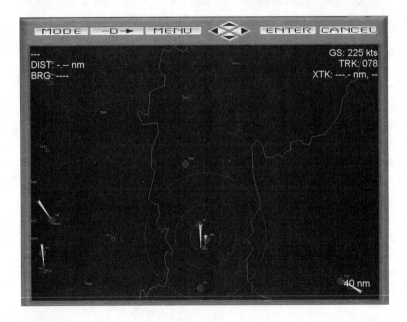

Figure 4.2 *The GPS displays your GS in the upper-right corner.*

Altimeter If your altimeter fails, you can still use your VSI (Vertical Speed Indicator) to maintain your current altitude. Keep the needle centered on the zero and maintain visual separation from the terrain. If you're in IMC, you might not be able to see the ground. In such a case, you can use navigation receivers to intercept an Instrument Landing System (ILS) glide slope, which will guide you safely down to a runway.

Attitude Indicator The attitude indicator (sometimes called the "artificial horizon") provides you with a concise representation of your aircraft's pitch and roll. Without this instrument, you can still look at the horizon outside the windscreen. The problem, of course, comes in low visibility, when you can't see the real horizon. You can work around this by paying attention to the turn coordinator (TC), VSI, airspeed, and heading indicators (HI). The turn coordinator displays rate of turn (see Figure 4.3), and if the VSI shows you

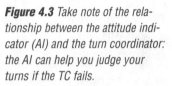

Figure 4.3 *Take note of the relationship between the attitude indicator (AI) and the turn coordinator: the AI can help you judge your turns if the TC fails.*

descending while you are at a reasonable airspeed, you're probably—but not necessarily—nose-down. If your heading indicator is drifting, you're probably rolled in the direction of the turn. Of course, you should also watch the altimeter for climbs and descents, which will give you some insight into your pitch if you're at standard controlled-flight airspeeds. By using the clues from all of these instruments, you can paint a reasonably complete picture of your plane's attitude, even in zero visibility.

Heading Indicator Driven by a powered gyro, the heading indicator gives you accurate readings on the direction your nose is pointing. If you lose this gauge, you can still find the information you're looking for on your compass. Be aware that the magnetic compass is most accurate during straight-and-level flight. During turns, descents, or airspeed changes, errors in the magnetic compass readings will occur. Note that you'll have to bring the compass up by selecting it under the View menu.

Turn Coordinator The turn coordinator shows rate of turn and quality of turn. The inclinometer (or "ball") that is located on the bottom half of the gauge shows if the plane is being flown in balance. It will never fail in the simulation. The top half of the gauge, the aircraft symbol and the placard that states a time (2 MIN), shows rate of turn. Bank so that either wing on the aircraft symbol lines up with the line below the wing-level line, and the plane will turn through 360 degrees in 2 minutes, 180 degrees in 1 minute. This part of the TC can fail in the simulation. The only substitute is timing your turns. You can approximate a standard-rate turn (three degrees per second) by using the AI to fly an appropriate bank angle for your current true airspeed to conduct a standard-rate turn.

You can also take your indicated airspeed, divide it by 10 and add half of this answer to arrive at the proper bank angle for a standard rate turn. For 100 knots indicated, the bank angle would be 15 degrees (100/10 = 10 + 5 = 15). Maintain that bank for a specific amount of time (for example, 30 seconds for a 90-degree turn, 1 minute for a 180-degree turn). Crosscheck your progress by noting the amount of heading change on the HI or compass and the amount of time that change required.

Vertical Speed Indicator   Your VSI is easily replaced by your altimeter. If the altimeter isn't moving, your rate of descent/ascent is zero.

Mechanical Failures

Mechanical and system failures are more severe than simple instrument malfunctions. Instead of a single gauge failing, the system that makes the gauge work has broken down. This usually affects multiple instruments, and may even make continued operation of the aircraft difficult.

Mechanical failures can affect the controls, impeding your ability to pilot the aircraft. The section below outlines each system and the instruments it affects, teaching you how to both identify and overcome failures.

Electrical   Your electrical system controls lighting, communication and navigation radios, and all digital systems. The first thing to do in the event of an electrical failure is to cycle the system by shutting down all electrical systems (lights, avionics, etc.), and then turning the master switch off and on. You may have inadvertently hit the switch, or you may have had a transient failure.

If you truly have lost electrical power, you'll lose all electrical systems, which is hard on a digital aircraft. On smaller, piston-powered aircraft such as the Cessna 172 and Cessna 182, the attitude indicator and heading indicator are vacuum driven, so fortunately you'll still be able to manage your aircraft's attitude when behind the controls of those planes. In other craft, unfortunately, without visual references you'll have no idea where you are or where you're headed. Descend slowly until you find a visual reference, and then set the plane down at the nearest safe location.

Engine   Single-engine aircraft will have no thrust whatsoever if the engine goes out, so you will immediately have to begin rationing your altitude for airspeed. Every aircraft has a published maximum glide speed, which is important to know and maintain when presented with an engine-out situation. Also, loss of thrust makes your aircraft more susceptible to departure in turns, because the speed lost in turns combined with the reduced vertical lift will naturally bring you closer to stalling. Therefore, be sure to take it nice and easy while banking, as shown in Figure 4.4. Sharp or sudden turns bleed airspeed, and since you have a limited amount, you can't afford to waste it. Descend as gradually as possible while maintaining your aircraft's published maximum glide range speed. When you find a suitable landing site, use a long and generous approach to avoid the need for violent maneuvering,

and try to land facing into the wind to lower your ground speed.

Losing an engine on a multi-engine airplane may seem less of an issue, but in reality is potentially more dangerous than in a single engine aircraft. Your plane won't lose thrust entirely, which can help you limp to a controlled landing, but control of the aircraft becomes more difficult. The most important thing to do is to cancel the severe induced yaw (using the rudder and bank procedure explained below) and use gentle, gradual control inputs. Whenever possible, avoid high AOA (Angle of Attack)— the angle at which air is flowing over the wing—by maintaining your airspeed above your aircraft's published minimum control airspeed (Vmc) at all times, and look for a place to set down.

Figure 4.4 *If you suffer engine loss, you must execute very gentle and gradual maneuvers to avoid losing speed unnecessarily.*

When one engine fails on a multi-engine plane during (or shortly after) takeoff, you will face some very serious challenges and decisions.

➤ If the engine failure occurs at or before liftoff, all throttles should be closed immediately and the takeoff aborted.

➤ If your airspeed is below the engine-out best angle of climb speed (Vxse) and the landing gear has not been retracted, the takeoff should be abandoned immediately.

➤ If Vxse has been obtained and the landing gear is in the process of being retracted, you should continue flight, landing as soon as safely possible. Maintain your heading with the rudder and continue to climb at Vxse to clear potential obstructions before stabilizing at the engine-out best rate of climb speed (Vyse), also known as "blue line" because of the blue line marking on the airspeed indicator.

Should the failure occur after achieving Vyse, then you should maintain your heading with the rudder and roll into a bank of at least five degrees toward the working engine to offset any asymmetrical torque resulting from the engine failure. Ensure that the working engine's mixture controls, prop controls, and throttle (in that order) are at their maximum permissible power settings and that the flaps and landing gear have been retracted.

> **NOTAM**
> **Notice to All Airmen**
>
> Remember, your primary goal in an in-flight emergency is the preservation of life onboard the aircraft and on the ground. Sometimes that goal may have the side effect of damaging the aircraft on landing. Life is always more important than property damage!

Once you've decided to continue flight rather than abort the takeoff, Vyse should be maintained even if altitude cannot be maintained. Even if that speed results in a descent, it will be at the slowest rate possible. Trading airspeed for altitude below Vyse will result in a self-defeating cycle in which you will eventually run out of airspeed. At airspeeds below the published Vmc speed, you risk losing directional control of the aircraft. If you are just barely able to maintain speed and altitude, maintain your bank angles under 15 degrees to avoid bleeding excess speed and altitude in turns. Look for a suitable landing site (your point or origin, an alternate airfield, or even a serviceable road or patch of open ground, depending on your options) as soon as your aircraft is under control.

Hydraulic Hydraulic pressure drives the control surfaces of many aircraft, as well as the wheel brakes. In such planes, loss of this system is critical, and it may result in disaster. The most important thing to do in the event of hydraulic loss is to maneuver slowly and gently. The following tips will help you compensate for the loss of any hydraulic system:

➤ **Ailerons:** You can compensate for aileron loss somewhat by using rudder and elevators. Rudders can induce and cancel roll, and your elevators can pull you through a turn. If you're in a twin-engine aircraft, lowering the thrust on one engine can drop that wing.

➤ **Brakes:** Loss of hydraulic pressure will likely affect your brakes, greatly increasing the aircraft's stopping distance on the runway. To avoid problems with this, land into a headwind on the longest runway available (divert to a large airport if one is available). Descend as slowly as possible to avoid building up speed. If your aircraft has thrust reversers, leave them deployed for as long as it takes to stop.

➤ **Elevators:** Elevator function can be replaced by your throttle and flaps. Increased throttle will increase your pitch, and flaps will affect your wing lift while also changing the location of the center of lift on the wing, causing a change in pitch attitude that can vary from plane to plane. On high-wing craft, extending flaps usually makes the nose pitch up, while on low-wing craft, extending flaps generally causes the nose to pitch down.

➤ **Flaps:** While experiencing hydraulic or electrical problems that affect the flaps, fly within the prescribed airspeed of whatever position in which your flaps are stuck. This may result in low cruising speeds if your flaps are down, or a high landing speed if your flaps are retracted. Again, remember that you might have degraded brake performance, so look for a long runway and set down on the stripes.

➤ **Rudder:** Multi-engine aircraft can use independent throttle adjustments to affect yaw. Single-engine aircraft can just do without it, using uncoordinated turns to replace rudder input.

Pitot-Static System The pitot tubes drive your aircraft's airspeed indicator. The system is also connected to the static ports, which drive the altimeter and VSI gauges. By measuring pressure differences, this system provides these gauges with the information that they display. If your pitot-static system goes down, these gauges will fail (see Figure 4.5). Use known settings of engine RPM to approximate airspeed. Use your GPS, your attitude indicator, and your autopilot's altitude function to replace these gauges, and try to maintain your altitude with visual reference and careful attention to the AI.

Figure 4.5 *Loss of your altimeter can be crippling in low-visibility situations.*

If your system fails, try toggling the pitot heat switch as problems are often caused by icing inside the pitot tube, which creates a blockage and disables the system. The heat switch warms the air inside the tube and can melt away the icy blockage. If this doesn't work, try descending into warmer air in the hopes of clearing the system. If your pitot system still doesn't respond, it may be something more severe than a blockage.

Radio Losing your radio system while under VFR (Visual Flight Rules) has very little effect, and you can safely land without being significantly endangered. Use the standard approach for aircraft that are out of communication with ATC when landing by observing the airport traffic pattern and entering when safe to do so. As soon as you can, establish visual contact with air traffic control, and land in turn when it is safe to do so. If you are on an instrument flight plan, but are in VMC (Visual Meteorological Conditions) and can maintain this favorable weather all the way to a suitable airport, land VFR. If you're in IMC (Instrument Meteorological Conditions), you're in greater peril. Fortunately, you still have the ability to monitor your aircraft's attitude, altitude, and airspeed. So as long as you are familiar with the area you're flying in, you should be able to avoid the terrain. Climb to at least 1,000 feet above any potential elevation (if you're operating under IFR, your assigned altitude or the published minimum en-route altitudes keep you clear of obstacles anyway) and look for a place to set down. If you can, try using landmarks or dead reckoning to navigate to a known airfield and execute a no-radio approach.

Check to make sure that you haven't turned the master electrical switch off if you lose your radios. Confirm that you're tuned to the proper frequencies if you're not getting radio response.

Vacuum The vacuum system drives your attitude and heading indicators. If you see these gauges fail together, you must completely ignore their readings. You won't see an immediate loss of function; as the vacuum pressure drops, the indicators will slowly "slough off" and eventually die. To avoid being fooled by this, you should routinely match your heading indicator to your compass reading during flight. If they don't jibe, you might be looking at a pump failure. Overcome the loss of your vacuum system just as you would the individual gauges—use your compass, altimeter, VSI, and turn coordinator to monitor your aircraft's attitude.

WARNING

Stalls don't happen without warning, so watch for hints from your aircraft. You'll experience a slight shudder (caused by the uneven flow of air over the wings striking the tail), a gradual loss of speed, and the controls will grow increasingly sluggish and unresponsive. At this point, you have a couple of seconds to reduce your angle of attack to avoid stalling the aircraft.

Pilot Error

Departures are almost always a result of pilot error, and their severity varies. The following sections will help you avoid and recover from departures.

Stalls Stalls come in many different degrees of urgency. A minor stall at altitude is simply a matter of lowering the nose and letting your airspeed increase above the stall speed. A stall just after takeoff is a potential catastrophe, because the aircraft has no time or space to recover before crashing to the ground.

A stall occurs when a wing does not generate enough lift to keep an airplane in controlled flight. This happens whenever the AOA (the wing's angle of attack) becomes so great that air begins to pull away from the top surface of the wing. This creates turbulence, which destroys the wing's ability to create lift (see Figure 4.6). No lift equals no fly, so keep your AOA within the performance envelope of your aircraft. For most of the aircraft in *Flight Simulator 2002*, that means using the airspeed indicator as an indirect measure of AOA and staying above the published stall speed for your aircraft. But even when you do exactly that, stalls can still happen at any airspeed and in any attitude, so be sure to study the excellent walkthrough of stall avoidance in Rod Machado's Ground School Handbook, included with your *Flight Simulator 2002* online documentation.

Figure 4.6 *Stalls can be fatal at low altitudes.*

To recover from a stall, reduce your AOA and increase your airspeed. Do this by pushing your throttle to maximum, releasing the amount of backpressure on the elevator, thus letting your nose drop and trading altitude for speed. Unfortunately, you probably got into the stall because you needed to do just the opposite—climb, and fast. No matter how low you are, you must let the nose settle down, or your rate of descent will only increase. If you're going to hit the ground, it's better to do it as slow and level as you can, so drop that nose to the horizon and hold on tight.

Spins Spins are more severe than stalls. In a stable aircraft (a term that can be applied to most private and commercial planes), it is supposed to be difficult to induce a

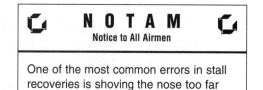

N O T A M
Notice to All Airmen

One of the most common errors in stall recoveries is shoving the nose too far below the horizon.

spin, though they can happen when the plane is mishandled in turns, stalls, or is flown at minimum controllable airspeeds. You're unlikely to encounter a spin at the controls of a Cessna, but they're more common in such aircraft as the Extra 300S (see Figure 4.7).

Figure 4.7 *It's easier to induce spins in the Extra 300S than in more stable aircraft.*

Often you'll stall the low wing first, and the nose will tend to move in that direction, dragging the aircraft into a spiral. When that happens, you can try to avert a spin by lowering the nose and applying opposite rudder. If you can keep the nose from yawing toward the low wing, the wing won't drop any farther before you break the stall. If that is unsuccessful and you enter a spin, the first things you should do are close the throttle and apply full opposite rudder, which should slow the rotation and neutralize the ailerons. Apply quick, forward movements of the elevator (push the yoke or stick forward) to decrease the excessive angle of attack and, hopefully, break the stall. Once you've done so, neutralize the rudder (if you don't, you may induce a second spin).

NOTAM
Notice to All Airmen

The rudder first, aileron second directions vary depending on the aircraft and type of spin. The actions generally occur almost simultaneously.

Once your spin is cancelled and your nose is pointing at the ground, gently pull back on the stick and climb to level flight, using your airspeed to help regain some of the altitude lost during the departure.

Recovering From Unusual Attitudes

One of the most common immediate results of any system failure or in-flight emergency is the aircraft's entry into an unusual attitude. An unusual attitude is any attitude that is not normally required for instrument flight and is generally unintentional and unexpected. As such, a surprised pilot flying in IMC may fall victim to an instinctual response in an attempt to recover, which may be inappropriate to the situation. The proper response is to act thoughtfully and deliberately according to established recovery procedures.

When you discover your aircraft is in an unusual attitude, you should immediately concern yourself with the recovery of straight-and-level flight, as opposed to trying to deduce how the aircraft got into the situation. First, you must learn to recognize an unusual attitude. Given airspeeds within an aircraft's safe flight range, nose-high attitudes are usually indicated by the attitude indicator, the rate of movement of the altimeter needle in the positive direction, a positive vertical speed indicator, and the airspeed indicator showing a decrease in airspeed. Nose-low attitudes are generally characterized by opposite instrument readings.

Once you have identified the unusual attitude, you must make the appropriate response. Rather than rely solely upon the attitude indicator, the pilot should gather a complete picture of the aircraft's situation from the airspeed indicator, altimeter, VSI, and turn coordinator. If nose high, increase power proportionally with the observed deceleration, apply forward elevator pressure to level the nose and avoid a stall, and level the wings with coordinated aileron and rudder pressure. Nose-low attitudes should be corrected by reducing power, correcting bank angle with coordinated aileron and rudder pressure, and applying smooth back pressure on the elevator only after the wings are level. Only reconsider the attitude indicator once the other instruments suggest the aircraft is close to level flight.

Aerobatics

Flight Simulator 2002 allows you to fly one of the world's most capable aerobatic aircraft, the Extra 300S. With a 300-horsepower engine, perfect design harmony, and legendary German engineering, this thoroughbred has been conquering international aerobatic competitions since its introduction to the marketplace in 1988. Flying the Extra 300s is a unique experience in *Flight Simulator 2002* because it is much more responsive than any of the other aircraft modeled in the simulator. Oversized control surfaces give you precise control over a 400-degree-per-second roll rate, instant response throughout the flight envelope, and an incredible amount of attitude control right up to the edge of its flight envelope. The thrust-to-weight ratio on the Extra is equally impressive, with the ability to "hang" the aircraft on the propeller for a time.

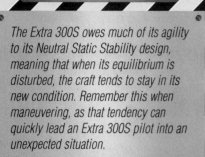

Aerobatics are not just for stunt pilots. Although you may not be crazy enough to try a Cuban Eight in your Learjet, the skills learned during such maneuvers can have universal applications. Energy management is part and parcel of aerobatic piloting, and the same concepts apply to normal flight. Learning to fly at or near your aircraft's stall speed is extremely useful for pilots and has direct applications in takeoff and landing procedures (see Figure 4.8). Getting a feel for the extreme limits of your aircraft's flight envelope is invaluable, as you'll develop a better sense of its capabilities and limitations. Better understanding leads to greater preparedness should you be faced with an emergency situation in flight.

Figure 4.8 *Every time you fly, you'll transition through your stall speed at least two times—on take-off and on landing.*

This section teaches you how to perform several aerobatic maneuvers using the Extra 300S. Before attempting these advanced moves, though, run through the Extra's checklist in Chapter 3: Aircraft and Checklists. Then take her up for a leisurely cruise around the airport to get used to the feel of the plane in normal flight. Avoid the temptation to step right into aerobatics with the Extra—it's a challenge to fly it in normal flight. The massive engine creates considerable torque-induced roll and yaw, especially in rapid power transitions. Learn how to use a light touch on the controls, as anything else can quickly lead you into a stall or spin. After some gentle familiarization, you're ready to conquer the skies with a little aerobatic action!

The Brainy Stuff

Any treatment of aerobatic maneuvers wouldn't be complete without an introduction to a few advanced flight concepts. If terms like G-forces, lift vectors, and induced drag roll off your tongue, you can probably skip this part. On the opposite end of the spectrum, if you don't know and don't care, then by all means move on to the individual maneuvers following this section. However, if you fall somewhere in the middle and are willing to learn a little, this slightly technical introduction will be very useful.

G-Forces

"G-force" is more than just the name of a great cartoon series. The term is short for gravity force, which can be thought of as the force or pull of gravity on the body, but is actually a measure of *acceleration*. The Earth's gravity is a constant acceleration of 9.8 m/s^2 (meters per second, squared) acting on everything.

While you don't feel like you're accelerating toward the ground, you do feel the weight of your body against the chair you're sitting in. Most people think of weight as a constant, as in, "I weigh 180 pounds." In reality, your weight is the product of your mass multiplied by your acceleration, in accordance with the formula: Force = Mass x Acceleration.

So in gravity's standard pull, you do weigh 180 pounds. You are currently experiencing 1G, which means one times the Earth's standard gravitational pull of 9.8 m/s^2. However, if that chair you're in were in an airplane that lifted into the sky at a constant acceleration of 9.8 m/s^2, you would be experiencing 2 Gs (one G for gravity and another G for the plane's acceleration), and the force pushing you into your chair would be twice what it is when you're sitting at your desk. You would suddenly seem to weigh 360 pounds!

Acceleration is a change in velocity, and velocity is a vector of speed and direction. Just as vertical acceleration exerts Gs to press you into your chair, horizontal acceleration (changing the direction vector by turning left or right) exerts Gs that push you left if you're turning right and vice versa.

So if you execute a gentle bank turn, you will exert very minimal G-forces on the aircraft, and they won't be very noticeable. By pulling back hard, a pilot can exert rapid acceleration along the plane's lift vector, which will induce G-forces on the plane. Conversely, you can push the nose down, which will actually induce negative Gs, pulling you up and out of your seat (see Figure 4.9).

TIP

Excessive G-loading bleeds speed and energy. Whenever you increase the G-forces on your aircraft, you slow down more than if you were under normal wing loads.

Figure 4.9 Negative Gs are induced by pushing the nose down and cause severe discomfort in real life.

These G-forces affect—and even define—the performance of your aircraft. Every aircraft has a different structural tolerance for G-forces. Light civilian aircraft can't handle more than a few Gs, while the Extra 300S can tolerate as many as 10 positive or negative Gs! This is truly impressive when you consider that the average person can only stay conscious through 5–6 Gs! If you exceed your aircraft's design tolerances, you can very easily depart the aircraft in dramatic fashion, damage control surfaces, or even rip the wings off the fuselage. Be sure to stay within the G loads that your aircraft was designed to handle.

Maneuvers

Each of the following maneuvers is described from beginning to end. By following along in the text, you should be able to successfully execute these aerobatic maneuvers with accuracy and finesse. Don't forget to record your flights so that you can watch your airborne expertise in replays!

NOTAM
Notice to All Airmen

If you intend to put on an "airshow," it's customary to execute all of your maneuvers above and parallel to the runway. In this way, you present spectators on the tarmac with the best possible viewing angle for your aerobatic display.

The Barrel Roll

Barrel rolls trace their lineage back to First World War air combat, in which they were used to gain position on an enemy fighter, or to bleed speed to maintain a trailing position. A normal aileron roll simply spins an aircraft about its long axis. A barrel roll is a corkscrew flight path that is centered around the plane's original axis of flight. Head-on, a barrel roll looks like the plane is stuck to the outside of a spinning barrel (thus the name), as seen in Figure 4.10.

Figure 4.10 *Executing a barrel roll requires elevator and aileron coordination.*

To execute a full barrel roll, pitch up 30 to 45 degrees, and then push the stick to one side while maintaining back pressure as well. The elevators will pull you up on your lift vector, and that vector will constantly rotate around the "barrel" as your ailerons roll the aircraft. Maintain steady pressure on the elevators and the ailerons to create a smooth corkscrew. When you complete 360 degrees of roll, you should be on your original heading. If you overshoot, increase your roll rate so that you come back to level faster. Undershoot, and you'll have too much roll or too little elevator.

You can also execute a half-barrel roll, which will only take you through a half-circle. Begin in straight-and-level flight, and then apply steady aileron and elevators. Let the aircraft roll over onto its back, and then cancel your elevators while continuing your aileron roll. You'll end up beside your original flight path, 90 degrees from your original heading.

The Chandelle

The Chandelle is a maximum performance climbing turn. In addition to the attractive smoke pattern that it leaves behind, this graceful maneuver is the most efficient way to execute a turn and climb at the same time, trading airspeed for a course change while netting maximum altitude gain. When completed properly, you'll turn 180 degrees and end in a nose-high attitude at the minimum control-

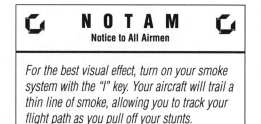

NOTAM
Notice to All Airmen

For the best visual effect, turn on your smoke system with the "I" key. Your aircraft will trail a thin line of smoke, allowing you to track your flight path as you pull off your stunts.

lable airspeed. The Chandelle requires very little wing loading, and as a result it can be performed by most of the aircraft in *Flight Simulator 2002*.

To execute a Chandelle, fly straight and level below your craft's published maximum entry speed. Begin the maneuver by rolling to a maximum performance bank angle, which varies by aircraft. As a rule of thumb, 30 degrees is the max. Once you are at your ideal bank angle, pull back gently on the stick, with the goal of maintaining the same bank angle throughout the first half of the maneuver while increasing pitch at a constant rate, achieving the highest pitch as you complete 90 degrees of the turn. Passing through 90 degrees, hold the pitch angle steady and begin steadily reducing your bank angle (see Figure 4.11). You may have to release a bit of back elevator pressure to keep the nose from rising. Coordinate your turn with the rudder, and bring the wings back to level when you've turned 180 degrees. You should be just above stall speed in level flight, heading in the opposite direction you started.

Figure 4.11 *Because of its low wing loading, many aircraft are capable of performing a Chandelle.*

The Cuban Eight

The Cuban Eight is a high-energy maneuver that traces the curves of an "8" lying on its side. The plane loops up and over onto its back to make one of the circles, and then rolls upright to repeat the maneuver, going the other direction to create the second circle. From the side, it looks like the plane has drawn the number 8!

A Cuban Eight is divided into two parts. The first half is five-eighths of a loop. You stop the airplane inverted on a 45 down line. You're inverted at this point and do a half roll to get upright. Then you duplicate the process for the second half—another five-eighths of a loop followed by an inverted 45 down line and a half roll to upright. The two looping parts have to be flown at the same altitude with the same radius, and the exit has to be at the same altitude as the entrance to the figure to create the lazy 8.

The Hammerhead

One of the more impressive airshow maneuvers is the Hammerhead. It's also known as a Hammerhead Stall or Stall Turn even though the plane never stalls (its airspeed does often approach zero). The plane zips along the flight line at low altitude and pulls up into a vertical climb, eventually coming to a near-stop at the top of the climb before a rudder turn rotates the nose back toward the ground so it can go back down the way it came.

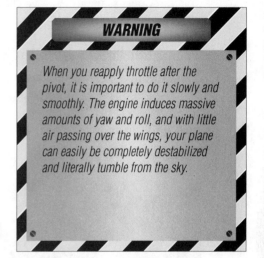

WARNING

When you reapply throttle after the pivot, it is important to do it slowly and smoothly. The engine induces massive amounts of yaw and roll, and with little air passing over the wings, your plane can easily be completely destabilized and literally tumble from the sky.

To execute a Hammerhead, begin in straight-and-level flight at a moderate speed. Pull up hard into a quarter loop for a vertical climb, using ailerons and rudder to maintain the line and plane's balance, then ease back on the throttle back a bit (smoothly, so that you don't stall the engine). Note that for some aircraft, such as the Extra, reducing throttle on the climb isn't necessary. When your airspeed gets down to about 20 knots, kick your tail over with full rudder to begin pivoting your nose (add a little opposite aileron to keep the plane from rolling at the top), then just before it's pointing straight down, apply rudder opposite the pivot (see Figure 4.12). As soon as your nose is pointing straight down, smoothly increase your throttle, and if needed use your ailerons. Let the plane drop straight down as you con-

Figure 4.12 *The Hammerhead is a guaranteed showstopper at any airshow!*

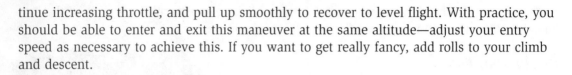
tinue increasing throttle, and pull up smoothly to recover to level flight. With practice, you should be able to enter and exit this maneuver at the same altitude—adjust your entry speed as necessary to achieve this. If you want to get really fancy, add rolls to your climb and descent.

The Immelmann Turn

This is a high-energy maneuver requiring considerable thrust and is not safely performable in most aircraft. The Immelmann is a half loop followed by a half roll so that you've reversed direction 180 degrees. You start low and fast, and end up flying in the opposite direction, higher and slower than your original flight vector (see Figure 4.13).

Figure 4.13 *An Extra 300S at the top of an Immelmann turn*

N O T A M
Notice to All Airmen

The Immelmann bears the name of its inventor, World War I German ace Max Immelmann. He used a slightly different technique (referred to as the "Combat Immelmann") in which he made an attack pass on an enemy at high speed, and then pulled straight up and out of reach. Before stalling, he would kick his nose around (similar to a Hammerhead) and make another attack run.

The Immelmann is fairly easy to execute in the Extra 300S. If you're trying this maneuver in a standard civilian aircraft, be sure to run your fuel mixture full lean to coax every last bit of horsepower out of the engine, and use a gentle descent before the maneuver to gain speed. In the Extra, begin in level flight at full throttle. Pull up smoothly through a half loop. Do not pull back too hard, or you'll bleed all of your energy entering the climb, setting you up for a stall. Once you're level at the top of the half loop, you'll be upside down, so execute a half-aileron roll to right the plane and exit the maneuver.

Part II
OVER THE
HORIZON

The wealth of features in Flight Simulator 2002 *makes this a truly expandable program. At their simplest, the powerful tools in the simulator allow you to create new flight plans and execute them under any conditions. Far deeper than that,* Flight Simulator 2002 *was created as a customizable platform, allowing pilot programmers to add to or change almost anything in the virtual world the simulation models. The following chapters will break down these powerful options so that even a casual simulator pilot can tailor his or her in-flight experience to personal taste.*

Chapter 5 teaches you how to create new flight plans and explains the rules and conventions governing them. Chapter 6 will teach you how to modify existing flight activities and share your entirely new adventures with your fellow virtual aviators.

CHAPTER 5
Creating a Flight Plan

A flight plan is essentially a summary of the details of any planned flight. In real life, pilots fill out a flight log before each flight, using information from charts, calculations from a flight computer, and information specific to their aircraft. Flight Simulator 2002 includes a powerful Flight Planner that automates the creation of a flight log, offering waypoint management, navaid information, and real-time mapping. This relieves the virtual pilot of all of the tedious flight planning work. The flight log generated by the Flight Planner also doubles as a flight plan for IFR flights. In this chapter, you'll learn how to create realistic flight plans.

Flight Plans in **Flight Simulator 2002**

A *Flight Simulator 2002* flight plan is a combination of a real flight plan and a flight log, which contains much more detailed information. When you generate your flight plan using the Flight Planner, a Navigation Log (NavLog) will be automatically generated that includes not only the route and its waypoints, but also distance, speed, estimated time en route (ETE), radio and navaid frequencies, and runway information. This comprehensive information greatly reduces your cockpit workload when you're airborne, and therefore it is an important part of serious simulated flying.

Initial Flight Planning

Flight planning begins with the essentials. Ask yourself about where you are coming from and where you will be going. The next question involves figuring out how you are going to get to your chosen destination. The first step is to take a look at the map—either in the World menu under Map View or within the Flight Planner itself—and check the distance between the two points. Now you must answer some more basic questions:

➤ Is the distance between your origin and destination safely within your aircraft's maximum range? FAA regulations require a 30-minute fuel reserve during the day and a 45-minute fuel reserve at night. If the trip is longer than your legal maximum range, you'll have to break it up into two or more legs with refueling stops in between.

➤ What navigation method are you going to use? Will this be a VFR (Visual Flight Rules) or IFR (Instrument Flight Rules) flight? If you are going to be using pilotage, you'll need to identify reasonably spaced landmarks along your route. If you intend to use navaids, you must identify useful transmission stations in your path. A GPS flight calculates a great circle route, giving you the shortest distance between your origin and destination.

➤ Is there any adverse terrain or special use airspace that must be flown over or avoided along your route?

➤ Are there any special limitations or conditions that will apply to the flight? Time constraints, inclement weather, specific overflight requirements, special aircraft considerations, or any number of other factors can affect flight planning, and they must be responsibly considered.

A check of the Weather menu will tell you what the current conditions are. Naturally, you can always arrange for clear skies and fair breezes, or you can specify any other sort of weather you wish. If you connect to the Internet, *Flight Simulator 2002* also offers you the ability to download and fly in the actual, real-world weather conditions that are currently affecting the area you are traveling through. This is not only realistic, but it also relieves you of the burden of creating realistic or complex weather patterns. Downloading real-world weather is as simple as a click of the mouse (see Figure 5.1).

Figure 5.1 *You can match meteor-ological conditions in the real world at the time of your virtual flight.*

Routing

When you have the basics of the flight established, it's time to dive into the Flight Planner and begin constructing your final route. The fastest way to do this is to enter your origin and destination airports in the Create tab of the Flight Planner dialog box, as shown in Figure 5.2, and then let *Flight Simulator 2002* automatically create a route for you. You can

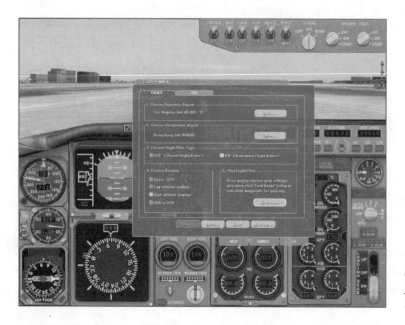

Figure 5.2 *Create Flight Plan allows you to generate a flight plan between any two airports.*

also generate a custom route of your own choosing. Both methods are described in the following sections.

Automatic Routing

When you have your origin, destination, and flight plan type established, it's time to choose a routing preference. The simulator will calculate a route between your origin and destination airports based upon one of the four methods described below:

> **Direct – GPS:** This method plots a great circle route directly between your origin and destination airports for use with GPS tracking. Your course will automatically be loaded into your GPS, allowing you to follow your track line with the GPS window open in the cockpit.

> **Low Altitude Airways:** Some VHF Omnidirectional Range (VOR) radials that are commonly traveled are designated as Victor airways. These are established flight corridors that are a specific type of controlled airspace. They not only lead from VOR to VOR, but can also lead to intersections between radials from two different stations. These intersections are uniquely named, and they will show up on a flight plan. By selecting this option, the Flight Planner will choose a route with a bias toward selecting Victor airways, up to 18,000 feet Mean Sea Level (MSL).

TIP

To see Victor airways (federal airways below 18,000 feet MSL) on the flight map, click the "V" icon on the right side of the toolbar at the top of the map. The airways will display as solid blue lines. To see the name of an intersection, just click it.

> **High Altitude Airways:** These "J" or jet routes are between 18,000 feet and 45,000 feet MSL, and any craft capable of such altitudes can use them. This option will create a flight plan based upon these high altitude airways.

> **VOR to VOR:** For shorter flights, or when moving along routes without established Victor airways running reasonably close to your desired course, it is sometimes easiest to fly directly from one VOR to the next. Flying VOR to VOR also avoids the use of Victor airway intersections, which involves radial interception from multiple VOR stations instead of just one at a time, and is therefore one step more complex than proceeding directly to a VOR station.

Once you've selected your routing preference, click Find Route to auto-generate a route. You'll be taken to the Edit Flight Plan screen, where your automatic route will be displayed, complete with waypoints listed on the right side of the map. From here, you can proceed to the NavLog section (see below).

Custom Routing

It is rewarding to select your own routing, as it puts you in direct control of your navigation choices. Also, you can choose indirect routes to your destination. This allows you to include anything from a scenic tour to a special-purpose waypoint for activities such as aerial photography, scientific reconnaissance, or any other reason. Also, you are more likely to have an intuitive sense of your flight plan if you personally choose each of the waypoints along the route.

N O T A M
Notice to All Airmen

When creating custom routes, it's easy to forget about the terrain! The Flight Planner map does not include any altitude information, so you'll have to refer to a sectional chart for that information. You can also use a third-party software program that includes this data. For more information, see the "FSNavigator" section in Chapter 9: Sharing the Sky.

To create a custom route, start with an auto-generated route. Select Direct – GPS routing, just to get a flight path drawn between your origin and destination. Once it is on the map, you can click and drag the line freely (as shown in Figure 5.3) to any navaid, intersection, or airport. Each time you click, drag, and release, a waypoint is created in the list on the right side of the screen. If you make a mistake, simply highlight the errant waypoint and click the Delete button at the bottom of the list.

Custom routes can use any combination of direct routing, Victor airways, or VOR-to-VOR routes that you desire. This added flexibility is another reason why custom routes are so useful. They do take more time, however, so if you're just interested in getting in the air as soon as possible, the automatic routing function won't steer you wrong.

Figure 5.3 *Drag the red flight path over any point on the map and release it to create a waypoint.*

Altitude

Altitude is obviously a critical consideration in any flight plan...the operative word is *flight*, after all! Several considerations will help you determine the optimal altitude range for your flight, as follows:

➤ **Terrain:** The ground level is the most obvious consideration in your altitude selection. It's generally accepted that most aircraft fly best when they are above ground level, and the FAA specifies minimum safe altitudes that must be observed (see sidebar). The lower you fly, the more inherent dangers there are, including many obstacles that can be hard to see. Also, flying at low altitudes reduces your options in the event of an emergency, such as a loss of thrust.

Minimum Safe Altitudes

Below is Federal Aviation Regulation (FAR) 91.119 (`http://www.access.gpo.gov/nara/cfr/`
`cfrhtml_00/Title_14/14cfr91_00.html`*), which declares the minimum safe altitudes for all aircraft not engaged in takeoff or landing procedures.*

(a) Anywhere. *An altitude allowing, if a power unit fails, an emergency landing without undue hazard to persons or property on the surface.*

(b) Over congested areas. *Over any congested area of a city, town, or settlement, or over any open air assembly of persons, an altitude of 1,000 feet above the highest obstacle within a horizontal radius of 2,000 feet of the aircraft.*

(c) Over other than congested areas. *An altitude of 500 feet above the surface, except over open water or sparsely populated areas. In those cases, the aircraft may not be operated closer than 500 feet to any person, vessel, vehicle, or structure.*

(d) Helicopters. *Helicopters may be operated at less than the minimums prescribed in paragraph (b) or (c) of this section if the operation is conducted without hazard to persons or property on the surface. In addition, each person operating a helicopter shall comply with any routes or altitudes specifically prescribed for helicopters by the Administrator.*

➤ **Clouds:** Clouds are often the determining factor in the maximum altitude available to a pilot flying under VFR, since you must stay at least 500 feet below the clouds. Sometimes, you may have room to climb up through a cloud layer, but if the clouds thicken, you'll have no way to get back down through them under VFR. Also, any such opening must be at least 4,000 feet across (a little under a mile) in order to be legal, as you are also required to maintain 2,000 feet horizontal separation under 10,000 feet MSL.

➤ **Weather:** Weather conditions also factor into prudent altitude selection. It's often best to climb above inclement weather, where it's bright and sunny no matter what's going on beneath the clouds. Higher is not always better, however, and sometimes pilots will descend to lower altitudes to drop out of turbulent atmospheric layers or avoid icing problems. Check the advanced weather conditions on your Weather menu, or consult the local ATIS (Air Traffic Information Service) channel for weather details.

➤ **Wind Speed:** In general, wind speeds are greater at higher altitudes. If you are flying into a headwind, you'll make better progress at lower altitudes. On the other hand, you can maximize your speed by ascending in a tailwind. There is a point of diminishing returns where the energy spent climbing is not made up by the increased tailwind at a higher altitude, so be aware of wind speed layers.

➤ **Flight Performance and Fuel Economy:** When selecting a cruise altitude, you should consider the length of the trip, your aircraft's climb performance, and fuel burn and true airspeed (TAS) at different altitudes. It doesn't make much sense to struggle up to 10,500 feet in a Cessna if you're only flying 100 miles. But if you want to fly 500 miles, the higher TAS and lower fuel burn at a the higher altitude may make sense, especially if you can ride a tailwind.

➤ **FAA Regulations:** The FAA has prescribed specific rules for VFR flight altitudes, similar to the IFR rules described in Chapter 3: Navigation. In general, from 3,000 feet Above Ground Level (AGL) to 18,000 feet MSL, aircraft flying a magnetic course between 0 and 179 degrees must fly at odd thousand-foot intervals, plus 500 feet. Examples of acceptable altitudes are 3,500, 5,500, and 7,500 feet. Aircraft headed the other way—from 180 to 359 degrees—must fly at even thousand-foot intervals plus 500 feet (4,500, 6,500, etc.). Note that these altitudes separate VFR traffic from IFR traffic by 500 feet. Use the mnemonic of NEOdd and SWEven to remember the even/odd rule (north and east, odd; south and west, even). For the full text of the Federal Aviation Regulations rules regarding VFR flight altitudes, see 95.159 at `http://www.access.gpo.gov/nara/cfr/cfrhtml_00/Title_14/14cfr91_00.html`.

The NavLog

One of the nicest luxuries in *Flight Simulator 2002* is that you don't have to deal with the complex calculations that go into the creation of a flight log. Finished real-world flight logs include information about electronic navigation (VOR frequencies, courses, intersections, and the like) as well as a complete set of dead reckoning (DR) calculations, which take into account magnetic variation, winds, indicated airspeed versus ground speed, time elapsed, and a host of other intricate factors. *Flight Simulator 2002* takes all of that work off your hands by automatically generating the Navigation Log (NavLog), as shown in Figure 5.4.

Figure 5.4 The NavLog at work

Using the NavLog

The NavLog presents a great deal of information in a concise format. If you aren't familiar with all of the concepts of flight planning, some of the brevity may seem confusing, which detracts from its usefulness as an in-flight tool and reference. This section will help you make heads and tails of the tables found on the NavLog by augmenting the information in the simulation's help documents.

Waypoints

Waypoints are the individual checkpoints along your route that allow you to generate a precise fix on your location. The Flight Planner that comes with *Flight Simulator 2002* can create waypoints at any established map feature, including VOR stations, airports, and established intersec-

The NavLog has a handy built-in print feature that will automatically send a formatted document to your printer with all of the information listed on your screen. Make use of it! It can be distracting to refer back and forth to the NavLog screen during flight.

tions. Each waypoint is displayed with its abbreviated three- or four-character International Civil Aviation Organization (ICAO) identification. The first waypoint is listed above the normal rows and represents your departure airport. Since you begin your flight there, you don't need the extra information that tells you how to get there!

If one of these ICAO ID names is unfamiliar to you, open up the Flight Planner and click the Edit tab. On the right side of the map, you'll find a list of all the waypoints on your planned route listed by ICAO ID and type. If you double-click one of these, it will be centered in the map window. Next, click the waypoint in the map, and it will call up a detailed description, as shown in Figure 5.5. The long description includes the full name of the VOR station, airport, or other map feature, allowing you to identify anything on the map and reconcile it with a chart or standard map.

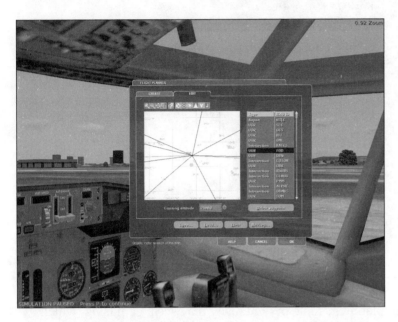

Figure 5.5 *The Flight Planner can display detailed information for any feature on the map.*

Many waypoints have a number listed next to their ICAO ID. This is the radio frequency of the navaid that the waypoint is based upon. To use the navaid, tune your NAV radio to the indicated frequency and use standard VOR and/or DME procedures to orient yourself to the station.

Route

The Route column indicates what type of route you have planned in order to reach the indicated waypoint. If you've defined a VOR-to-VOR route, you'll see the "direct" symbol. If you've chosen an airway routing, you'll see the airway designator.

Altitude (Alt)

Altitude on each leg of your trip is displayed in feet MSL and represents the altitude you should maintain while en route to the associated waypoint. The proper route altitude is based upon whether you selected VFR or IFR in the Create Flight Plan screen. VFR altitude is determined by the terrain and the cloud level along your route. IFR altitude is determined by the Minimum En Route Altitude (MEA) requirements for your selected route. Naturally, both are generally regulated by the NEOdd/SWEven rule (see above). For detailed information on IFR altitude requirements, see FAR 91.177 at `http://www.access.gpo.gov/nara/cfr/cfrhtml_00/Title_14/14cfr91_00.html`.

Heading (Hdg)

Heading is the true course you should fly, in order to reach the given waypoint from the last waypoint in the list. Note that if you did not reach your last waypoint exactly, your actual required heading to reach the waypoint will differ.

Distance (Dist)

Distance is divided into two rows for each waypoint. All units are in nautical miles. The top row provides the length of the individual leg of the flight, which is to say the distance between this waypoint and the last. The second number is a measure of the total distance remaining on your flight after you reach this waypoint. If you find yourself with low fuel, this second number is an important aid in estimating whether you have enough fuel to complete your flight without a stop. Note that the first number, highlighted above the waypoint rows, is the total distance remaining to your destination from your current position.

Ground Speed (GS)

The Ground Speed (GS) column is measured in knots and expresses your speed over the ground—you can also think of it as your true airspeed corrected for the effect of a headwind or tailwind. As described in Chapter 4: Spreading Your Wings, your ground speed is usually different from your indicated airspeed (IAS). The NavLog provides you with two rows for each waypoint. The first is the estimated ground speed given your aircraft's cruising speed, and the second is left blank for you to fill in the actual speed achieved over each leg. You can compute this easily by dividing the listed distance of each leg by the number of hours it takes you to complete it. Thus, a 200-nautical-mile distance covered in two hours indicates a GS of 100 knots.

Fuel

This column measures the estimated fuel burn over each leg of the trip, given the listed altitudes and speeds. The highlighted first number underneath the column head displays the total gallons of fuel remaining in your aircraft's tanks. Compare this to the Fuel Total underneath the table—if your initial fuel is lower than your total fuel required, you can't complete the trip! In each waypoint row, the top box lists the estimated gallons of fuel required to complete the leg, while the bottom is left blank for you to fill in with the actual fuel burn.

TIP

Of course you've planned your flight so that you'll have adequate fuel reserves and checked your fuel burn early in the flight and periodically along the way by comparing your fuel remaining with what is required for the next leg of your trip. If you're burning more than expected, it's time for a fuel stop!

Time

The first (highlighted) number in this column is the flight time elapsed since your engine start, while the remainder of the column shows two boxes for each leg of your journey. The top box for each waypoint is the ETE, which is an approximation of the time it will take you to fly the leg of the trip leading up to that waypoint from the one immediately preceding it. The lower box is the actual time en route, or ATE. This is left blank for you to fill in as you reach each waypoint. Real flight logs also include ETA and ATA, which are clock times for recording your estimated and actual times of arrival at each waypoint.

CHAPTER 6
Expanding Existing Flights

Activities in Flight Simulator 2002 *will take you from realistic general aviation scenarios all the way to commercial captaincy guiding a jumbo jet. Even with this epic progression, the simulation's included activities are only the beginning of your potential adventures. This chapter teaches you how to create new activities, embark upon virtual flight careers, and even design entire sets of activities like the career scenarios that come with the simulator. These new challenges can be shared with other* Flight Simulator 2002 *pilots, ensuring an infinite supply of new horizons.*

Creating New Flights

The fundamental building block of new flight activities is the creation of a new flight. The powerful Flight Planner included with *Flight Simulator 2002* allows you to create a flight plan consisting of many steps. In addition to a flight plan's origin, destination, and way-points, a fully featured new flight includes aircraft selection, specific weather conditions, the time of day, and any other specific settings you'd like to include.

The Flight Concept

The first step in creating a new flight is to decide what you're trying to accomplish with its basic features. An infinite variety of experiences can be enjoyed in the virtual skies, and it's up to you to determine what conditions you want to simulate with your new flight (see Figure 6.1). The following areas are good starting points in the creation of your flight concept. Choose the one that is the most important element of the flight you have in mind and then adapt the others to fit your choice.

Figure 6.1 *You can create a flight dealing with just about any situation imaginable.*

After you've gone through these considerations and found one or more core concepts for your flight, balance these with the other variables. For example, if you've decided to simulate an engine failure to experiment with solving an emergency in flight, you need to choose between the multi-engine and single-engine planes. This selection will better define the complexity of the emergency.

Aircraft

Creating a flight that shows off the specific features of a particular aircraft makes for a straightforward starting point. The more unique the aircraft, the better. For example, the Bell 206B JetRanger III is the only aircraft in the simulator capable of hovering, making low-speed maneuvers, and landing on unprepared surfaces, while the Schweizer SGS 2-32 sailplane is the only glider in the *Flight Simulator 2002* stable. You can also create a flight that showcases the go-anywhere capabilities of the Cessna 208B Caravan or the long-range passenger service of the Boeing 777-400.

Area

A specific region of operation is an excellent basis for a new flight. The Grand Canyon's awe-inspiring cliffs, the searing heat of the Gobi Desert, the concrete jungles of a Hong Kong to Tokyo flight, or the breathtaking heights of an Alps crossing all offer unique flight experiences. Select a place that you have heard about, studied, or longed to travel to, and create a flight that showcases the most notable features of that region.

> ### NOTAM
> **Notice to All Airmen**
>
> New flights based around your hometown (or the airport that you usually operate out of in real life) can be very rewarding. With satellite map data and accurate depictions of almost every registered airfield in the world, *Flight Simulator 2002* offers you a new perspective on familiar territory.

Area challenges can also include airports themselves. Perhaps you'd like to try the challenge of operating at a major international airport such as Los Angeles International or John F. Kennedy in New York. The procedures and communications around these airports can provide a challenging and exciting flight.

Emergencies

You can create a flight designed to test you with a specific in-flight failure. Try an engine failure on takeoff or a hydraulic failure in flight. Gear problems on approach will help you practice belly landings. Any number of failures or in-flight emergencies can be made more exciting by a suitably tailored flight.

Environmental Conditions

Mother Nature is the ultimate authority on flight clearance, and thanks to the safety afforded by a simulator, you can fly in conditions you'd never attempt in real life. Try landing in zero visibility, or practice finding the best altitude to cross over a storm (see Figure 6.2). You can even create hurricane-force storms and experience the nail-biting challenge of the science teams that fly into these monsters to gather research data!

Figure 6.2 *You can base exciting flights on specific environmental conditions for practice or challenge.*

Time of day is also a relevant consideration. For example, try a forced landing on a runway at dusk, with the sun in your eyes. You can also adjust the season—don't forget that temperature is another part of the weather. A very hot day at high altitude makes for lower pressures, which dramatically alter the performance of an aircraft.

Occupations

Some piloting jobs are exclusive experiences, as a result of rigorous job requirements, occupational hazards, or even the outright scarcity of certain positions. Only a small number of pilots in the real world operate fire tankers, search-and-rescue planes, police helicopters, and numerous other vehicles, but you can take up these challenges any time thanks to *Flight Simulator 2002*. In these flights, your focus should be on creating a scenario true to whatever job you'd like to simulate, including proper aircraft, location, and procedures.

Special Scenarios

A role-playing challenge or special condition can be the focus of a flight. For example, you can simulate a high-powered executive's complex meeting schedule on the helipads of New York skyscrapers, or conduct low-altitude passes for a team of scientists observing a volcano. You can create a U.S. Border Patrol mission, in which the objective is to intercept a computer-controlled plane at the border and escort it to its destination, wherever that might be. These special scenarios do not have any associated game settings, but they can be fully described in the flight briefing.

As with the other concepts, choose the rest of your settings based upon your scenario. Low visibility makes searching harder, and an aircraft with a low top speed isn't the best choice for a pursuit. Take each factor into consideration as you make your selections and then create the flight, choosing settings that combine to make a complete and unified scenario.

Building the Scenario

When you have settled upon the general concepts guiding your new flight, it's time to start building it. The first step is the creation of a flight plan. First, decide where the flight is going to originate based on the choices made in the design phase. Open up the Flight Planner and select an airport from the Departure Airport dialog box (see Figure 6.3). Next, select the destination airport in the Destination Airport box.

Figure 6.3 *Select your departure and destination airports in the Flight Planner to begin building your new flight.*

As mentioned in the Real World Training Handbook included with the simulator, the flight doesn't have to start at the airport. Just the same, it's good to have a flight plan each time you take to the skies. This is particularly important in programmed activities, so that the pilot has something to refer to in flight. *Flight Simulator 2002* activities are not judged by the program itself, so the pilot's only way of knowing if the activity was completed successfully or not is by his or her own assessment. Including a flight plan provides the pilot with something upon which to base that assessment.

Creating the Navigation Log

Now that you have beginning and end points for your flight path, have the Flight Planner auto-generate a route for you using GPS (Direct) routing. This will place a straight line between your departure and destination airports. As described in Chapter 5: Creating a Flight Plan, you can click and drag the line to any map object to establish a waypoint. Set up the route to the desired specifications and then save the flight plan with the same name as your activity.

Single Airport Operations

If you are departing from and returning to the same airport, you'll have to take some additional steps in order to create a flight plan that includes waypoints. Since the Flight Planner won't generate a course line that can be manipulated for flights that begin and end at the same airport, you'll have to perform additional edits to the .PLN file (the file used to store the flight plan) using a text editor like Windows Notepad.

Start by selecting the airport you wish to use as your departure airport, then pick any nearby airport as the destination. Next, build your entire flight plan as you intend it to be, leaving the last waypoint at the undesired destination airport you chose (for now). Save the flight plan under the same name as your activity and exit Flight Simulator 2002.

Now, use Windows Explorer to open up the `Flights/Myflts` *subdirectory in your* `FS2002` *main directory. Open the .PLN file you just created with your text editor. At the end of the file, you'll see lines that identify your departure airport, your destination airport, and a list of all waypoints. Change the* `destination_id` *line to match the* `departure_id` *line, and also change* `destination_name` *to match* `departure_name`. *Lastly, change the last waypoint in the list to match the information in the first* `waypoint.0` *line, preserving only the number of this last waypoint. When finished, these lines should look like the following example of a roundtrip out of Los Angeles International (KLAX).*

```
departure_id=KLAX, N33° 56.15′, W118° 25.13′,
   +000126.00departure_position=7L
destination_id=KLAX, N33° 56.15′, W118° 25.13′,
   +000126.00departure_name=Los Angeles Intl
destination_name=Los Angeles Intl
waypoint.0=KLAX, A, N33° 56.15′, W118° 25.13′, +000126.00,
waypoint.1=KLAX, A, N33° 56.15′, W118° 25.13′, +000126.00,
```

Setting up the Flight

After your navigation log has been completed, it's time to create the rest of the scenario. Aircraft selection, weather configuration, selecting the time of day, tuning the radios, and all the other details of the activity must be set according to your design. It's acceptable to alter your design at this point if you have a better idea than what you originally planned. Just make sure to keep your core concept in mind and make only changes that support the original focus of the activity.

If weather isn't a critical factor in the activity, you can leave it clear. Better yet, have the activity use real-world weather by selecting the option in the Advanced Weather menu.

Slew the plane into the position you want it to begin the activity, as shown in Figure 6.4. If you want to start the activity in-flight, you can't use the slew commands straight off the ground because the simulation remembers not only your position, but also your airspeed. Therefore, fly to the position you want and pause the simulation when your aircraft is at the proper attitude and airspeed.

Figure 6.4 *Slew the aircraft to the ramp area for a realistic start to any flight.*

Configuring the Simulation

With everything else in place, finish your construction phase by configuring the simulation settings according to your flight design. Saved flights override user preferences for things such as reliability, time of day, weather, and other settings—unless a pilot specifically configures the simulation. Therefore, your flight settings will define the way that the activity is conducted every time it is flown. For example, if you specify a system failure, the system will fail even if a pilot's settings are normally set on 100% reliability.

Now that you've set up the simulation to match your design goals, save the flight (go to the main menu and choose Flights, then Save Flight). All files will be saved in the `FS2002/Flights/MyFlts` folder.

Creating New Activity Series

So far, you've built a comprehensive standard flight, essentially the same as the ones you can create on the spot for an individual flight session. The next step is to manipulate the files so that your flight becomes a full-fledged activity, complete with a flight briefing and an association with a flight series. This requires some technical work with data files outside of the simulation itself. The following steps will guide you through the process of creating a new activity group.

Preparing the Directory

The first step is to create a flight subdirectory. Create a new folder in the `FS2002/Flights` directory, and name it using some convention that helps you remember its contents. For example, the Desert Adventure series of flights are contained in the `DsrtAdv` folder. Use a folder name of eight characters or fewer to adhere to the same format as the activities that ship with the game.

When you have finished with your new folder, create a plain text document using your text editor (typically, WordPad). Within it, you should include three lines with the following labels:

```
[ MAIN]
Title=your title here
Description=your description of this flight series
```

The title should represent all of the flights that will be included in this flight series. The description, similarly, should be an overall description of the flights you are going to put in this folder. *Flight Simulator 2002* comes with several careers, each with numerous individual flights. You may choose to group your flights in any manner you wish; career is not the only way to go. For example, you may group your flights by region, aircraft, date of creation, or any other method that is convenient. Whatever you choose, make sure that the title and description help you identify the flights in this folder.

Save the text file under the file name `desc.txt` in your new folder. Make sure it is saved in plain text format (word processors and similar programs usually do not save their files in a format that can be used by the simulator).

Preparing the Flight Files

All saved flights are located in the `MyFlts` folder, which consists of .FLT, .PLN, and .WX files. The .FLT file is the flight file, which contains the basic scenario information, including all the settings you made to the simulation and the situation at the start of the activity. The .PLN file covers your flight plan, including all of the waypoints and navigation data used by the Navigation Log and Flight Planner. The .WX file deals with weather, which naturally contains all of the meteorological information.

Usually, the flight plan file will be named after the departure and destination airports (for example, `Los Angeles Intl to John Wayne.PLN`). Note that this may not match your actual flight plan, if you modified the destination airport to match the departure airport. You can rename the plan file to match your flight and weather files, but you must also edit the filename callout in the flight file. To do this, open the flight file and look for the section header marked `[GPS_Engine]`. The first line, `Filename=`, should be edited to reflect the new name of your plan file. You don't have to specify a path if the plan file is in the same directory as your flight file (which this procedure assumes).

Creating the Briefing

There is no provision for creating preflight briefings from within the simulator, but they are easily composed using a text editor. The briefings that come with *Flight Simulator 2002* use the same format, outlined below. If you want the flights to look like professional components of the simulator, you can use the same format. Of course, you can also create another style that conveys all the important flight information to the reader. The entire contents of your file will be displayed in the simulator briefing exactly as you type them, as shown below:

➤ Flight Series Title

➤ Flight Name

➤ Estimated Time to Complete

➤ About the Flight

➤ Required Knowledge/Skills

➤ The Weather

➤ Recommended Charts

➤ The Route

➤ Notes

TIP

The briefing file is your greatest tool in the creation of a new activity. Use it to define all the goals and features of your flight that cannot be conveyed through the flight plan. A clear, comprehensive, and engaging briefing is the heart of a new flight activity.

Use the briefing file to outline the parameters and goals of the flight. You can be as straightforward or as creative as you wish. The inclusion of a briefing allows you to create a flight that goes beyond even the configuration tools available within the simulator, giving you the power to create goals that are only limited by your imagination. Make sure that you describe the flight goals clearly and concisely, so that pilots who fly the activity will be able to understand and follow your directions.

After you have created the briefing file, save it as a plain text document, using the same name as your saved flight. Make sure that you specify the extension of .BRF instead of .TXT, so that the simulator will interpret it as a briefing file and display it properly (see Figure 6.5). If the name does not match that of your new flight file exactly, it won't load when you select the flight.

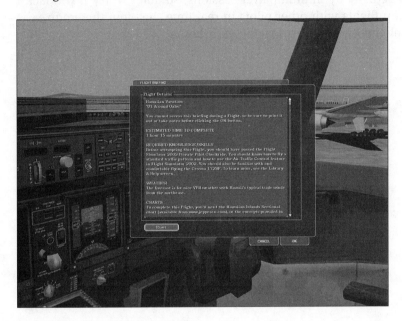

Figure 6.5 *The briefing file describes the background and goals of your new flight activity.*

Virtual Airlines

The Getting More documentation included on the *Flight Simulator 2002* CDs contains some information on virtual airlines. These groups of dedicated simulator pilots form real organizations of simulated airline businesses or organizations. Typically, these virtual airlines simulate passenger operations of all sizes, from commuter or regional service all the way up to international flights. However, virtual airlines are also modeled after cargo operations, specialized charter services, or even military groups.

Your *Flight Simulator 2002* adventures can be greatly enhanced by the shared challenges offered in the virtual airline environment. These player-run organizations are almost always operated free of charge, and they usually

N O T A M
Notice to All Airmen

In addition to the obvious advantages of the prepared flights and supplemental materials offered by virtual airlines, don't underestimate the value of belonging to a close-knit group of *Flight Simulator* fans. Most of these virtual pilots are quite experienced, and they'll be eager to help one of their own with answers, solutions, or suggestions.

offer many high-quality add-ons that will expand your flight experience. Usually, each flight completed will earn points that contribute to your personal totals. These points are usually applied toward seniority within the group, often represented by ranks.

The following links will help you find some virtual airlines online. Note that most virtual airlines do not require you to actually fly in multiplayer sessions, so don't worry if you lack the time or inclination to set up flights with other pilots in real time. Just join the group, download the associated supplements, and start logging your hours!

➤ www.va-center.com

➤ www.vuscg.org

➤ www.geocities.com/c5keeper/menu.htm

Part III
CONQUERING
THE SKIES

Flight Simulator 2002 *ships with a number of exciting flight activities, found on the Select a Flight menu off the main screen. These flights put you in the pilot's seat on flights that are based upon the kind of situations that real-world pilots face every day. From chauffeuring an author around New England in a light plane to flying commercial routes between international airports in a jumbo jet, the activities will give you an abundance of experiences through a wide variety of realistic flights. In Chapters 7 and 8, we'll provide you with all the reference materials you'll need to complete these flights successfully and walk you through the rough spots to help you reach your destination safely.*

In addition, we've included a whole chapter on multiplayer flights and activities. Multiplayer activities are among the most realistic applications of Flight Simulator, and no matter if you are an Internet novice or a multiplayer master, you'll find new ways to fly with other people through Chapter 9's easy and detailed explanations.

CHAPTER 7
Going Solo

This chapter provides you with tips and walkthroughs for each of the general aviation activities new to Flight Simulator 2002. Please note that you may find some advanced concepts below, as you are expected to have a full working knowledge of the concepts discussed in the previous chapters of this book. The following sections are organized for easy reference, so that you can flip directly to the passage explaining a concept that you don't understand. In this way, the activities can provide you with a kind of programmed instruction, teaching you applied skills on the fly (literally).

Aerial Chauffeur

Area: Northeastern United States

Aircraft: Cessna 182S

Flights: 7

Difficulty: Hard

The Aerial Chauffeur activities put you in command of a well-equipped Cessna 182S, owned by an eccentric author of mystery novels who lives on Nantucket Island in Massachusetts. After he grew weary of taking the ferry to and fro, he bought the plane on a whim and hired you to be his personal pilot. It's a good life in this New England haven, but you're on call 24 hours a day. Worse still, the author has no respect for the weather, and he "wants to go when he wants to go." The upshot is that you'll be logging lots of Instrument Flight Rules (IFR) flight time in this position, and you'll grow accustomed to many of the airways in New England.

Flight One: Booksigning in Provincetown

Origin: Nantucket Memorial (KACK), Nantucket, MA

Destination: Provincetown Municipal (KPVC), Provincetown, MA

Estimated Time En Route: 45 minutes

Time of Day: Morning

Weather: Overcast

Flight Plan: IFR

Route: ACK GAILS KPVC

Altitude: 5,000 feet

Landing: ILS Runway 7

Your first experience with your new boss involves ferrying him to a booksigning in Provincetown, Massachusetts, on the northern end of Cape Cod. A relatively light and steady eight-knot wind at 66 degrees gives you a bit of a headwind, but you can climb above it at 2,000 feet above ground level (AGL). It's an overcast day, and you'll be ducking in and out of the middle cloud layer at 5,000 feet. Generous visibility to 10 miles makes it a nice day for a flight, overall.

Radio Information

Nantucket Memorial (KACK)

STATION	FREQUENCY
Ground	121.70
Tower	118.30
Departure	126.10

Provincetown Municipal (KPVC)

Approach	118.20
CTAF	122.80
AWOS	119.025

NAV Radios

NAVAID	TYPE	FREQUENCY	DESIRED HEADING
ACK	VOR	116.20	349 (FROM)
PVC	NDB	389.0	50 (TO)
IVQO	ILS	111.10	75 (TO)

The Flight

Run through your start-up checklist, making sure to tune your radios. When you're ready, request takeoff clearance for an IFR departure. Ground clearance will assign you a runway; taxi to it, take off, and contact departure control when instructed. Your first waypoint is the ACK VHF Omnidirectional Range (VOR), on a heading of 60 from the airport. When you are within a mile of the VOR, reset your Omni Bearing Selector (OBS) to fly a "FROM" heading of 349 and maintain this course (tracking FROM the ACK 349 radial) for 39 DME (Distance Measuring Equipment) until reaching the GAILS intersection (see Figure 7.1). You'll have to cheat to the right a little bit with your heading in order to beat the crosswind blowing you to the left.

Use the time tracking the 349 radial to set up your radios for the approach. Tune in the localizer and set the inbound course on the OBS. Tune in the PVC non-directional radio beacon (NDB) with your automatic direction finder (ADF). Tune to KPVC AWOS (automated weather) on your COM2 radio to get the latest local conditions.

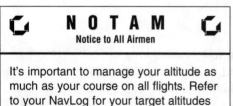

N O T A M
Notice to All Airmen

It's important to manage your altitude as much as your course on all flights. Refer to your NavLog for your target altitudes on each leg of your flight. In some cases, you will have to start ascending or descending before a waypoint in order to be at your next target altitude in time, so be sure to plan ahead.

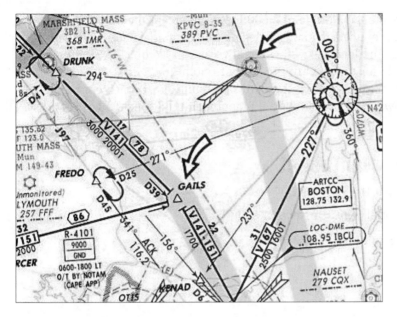

Figure 7.1 *The GAILS intersection*

Upon reaching 39 DME on the 349 radial, Approach issues you a new clearance: "Fly heading 030 degrees, descend and maintain 2,000 feet until established on the IVQC localizer, and cleared for the ILS to runway 7 at Provincetown. Change to local advisory frequency approved." You can now tune COM1 to the KPVC traffic channel on 122.80 and announce your position on the approach (shown in Figure 7.2). Since KPVC is an uncontrolled airport, you must announce and coordinate your landing intentions with other traffic in the area.

Figure 7.2 *You must announce your intentions to other pilots in the area at uncontrolled airports.*

As you descend to your clearance altitude of 2,000 feet to intercept the inbound localizer course of 075 degrees, notice the nice, standard 45-degree intercept angle you have been given by your controller. Since the localizer will come alive and move quickly, use the trick of monitoring your ADF needle for the head of the arrow to point to 75 degrees—your intended inbound course. Begin a progressive standard rate right turn to intercept the localizer course of 075 at this. Now, just fly a standard ILS approach until touchdown. Easy! (Right?)

Flight Two: Back to Nantucket

Origin: Provincetown Municipal (KPVC), Provincetown, MA

Destination: Nantucket Memorial (KACK), Nantucket, MA

Estimated Time En Route: 45 minutes

Time of Day: Noon

Weather: Overcast

Flight Plan: IFR

Route: KPVC LFV V167 GAILS V141 GROGG WAIVS KACK

Altitude: 7,000 feet

Landing: ILS Runway 24

After the booksigning, you fly back home to Nantucket. It was a short engagement, so the weather conditions are unchanged. On this flight, you'll enjoy a tailwind, which will help you make good time. You'll be using a Victor airway (V141) on this flight, which is a standard flight corridor.

Radio Information

Provincetown Municipal (KPVC)

AWOS	119.025
CTAF	122.80
Departure	118.20

Nantucket Memorial (KACK)

STATION	FREQUENCY
Approach	126.10
Tower	118.30
Ground	121.70

NAV Radios

NAVAID	TYPE	FREQUENCY	DESIRED HEADING
LFV	VOR	114.70	227 (FROM)
ACK	VOR	116.20	169 (TO)
AC (WAIVS)	NDB	248	Direct
IACK	ILS	109.10	241 (TO)

The Flight

Go through your start-up checklist and tune your radios. Provincetown is uncontrolled, so instead of asking someone for clearance, you just have to announce your intentions to the other pilots in the area and make sure there are no potential conflicts.

Your departure clearance for the return trip has you doing a little more work with VOR navigation. Upon takeoff, turn direct to the Marconi VOR (114.7). Remember: rotate the OBS ring until you get the needle centered with a "TO" indication. Upon reaching the VOR, turn southwest and track FROM the VOR on the 227 radial on the Victor highway V167. Climb and maintain 7,000 feet while tracking outbound on the 167 radial. Upon intercepting the Nantucket VOR 349 radial (Victor highway V141-151), turn left and track TO the 169 radial of Nantucket VOR (116.20).

Upon reaching 12 DME from the ACK (Nantucket) VOR at the GROGG intersection, Approach issues you a new clearance: "Turn left heading 120, maintain 1,600 until established on the localizer, clear for the ILS 24 approach at Nantucket. Contact the tower on 118.3." Upon contacting Nantucket tower, tower advises you: "Upon reaching 10.5 DME from IACK (the localizer) to turn right to a heading of 195 degrees to intercept the localizer, clear to land!"

Flight Three: Interview in Providence

Origin: Nantucket Memorial (KACK), Nantucket, MA

Destination: Green State Airport (KPVD), Providence, RI

Estimated Time En Route: 45 minutes

Time of Day: Noon

Weather: Broken clouds

Flight Plan: IFR

Route: KACK ACK V146 MVY PVD KPVD

Altitude: 6,000 feet

Landing: ILS Runway 5

A mystery writer's life is never dull. Consequently, neither is the life of a mystery writer's private pilot. Hearing word of a woman in Providence who claims that her house is haunted, your boss has set up an interview there. Naturally, you'll be the one taking him to the appointment.

Radio Information

Nantucket Memorial (KACK)

STATION	FREQUENCY
Ground	121.70
Tower	118.30
Departure	126.10

Green State (KPVD)

CONTROLLER	FREQUENCY
Center	124.85
Approach	135.40
Tower	120.70
Ground	121.90

NAV Radios

NAVAID	TYPE	FREQUENCY	DESIRED HEADING
ACK	VOR	116.20	60 (TO)
MVY	VOR	114.50	299 (TO)
PVD	VOR	109.10	312 (TO)
IPVD	ILS	109.30	47 (TO)

The Flight

This flight is relatively straightforward, with handy "TO" vectors on all legs direct to VOR/DME stations. A single layer of broken clouds extends from 3,000 to 7,500 feet. If you wish, you can alter your flight plan to take you above the weather, which would result in a safer flight (see Figure 7.3).

Green State is a controlled airport with Class C airspace, so take advantage of its radar service as early as possible. On approach, you'll be given vectors to intercept the glide slope,

Figure 7.3 *Modifying your flight plan to account for the weather makes good sense.*

and you'll probably be cleared direct, avoiding the need to enter a traffic pattern. Green State is the busiest airport in Rhode Island, so you should try to follow air traffic control's (ATC) directions as closely and as quickly as possible. A successful landing at Green State completes this flight.

Flight Four: Meeting in Boston

Origin: Green State Airport (KPVD), Providence, RI

Destination: Logan International (KBOS), Boston, MA

Estimated Time En Route: 45 minutes

Time of Day: Noon

Weather: Broken clouds

Flight Plan: IFR

Route: KPVD PVD V146 FOSTY V3 BOS KBOS

Altitude: 7,000 feet

Landing: ILS Runway 22L

After the interview with the haunted house lady, your employer has to head to Boston for a meeting with his publisher. Grab some lunch at the airport today, since

TIP

Seeing other planes in the air is a very enjoyable experience in Flight Simulator 2002. *If your frame rates are too low when you turn on air traffic in this flight, try turning down your detail levels one step, so that you can interact with other planes over Boston.*

you're not returning directly to Nantucket. Boston's Logan International is the largest airport you'll fly into in this activity series, so it will be a bit exciting to interact with the other planes in the air. You'll be flying Victor airways to Boston, to help navigate the crowded skies in this heavily populated area.

Radio Information

Green State (KPVD)

STATION	FREQUENCY
ATIS	124.20
Ground	121.90
Tower	120.70
Departure	126.10

Logan International (KBOS)

CONTROLLER	FREQUENCY
Approach	118.25 / 120.60 / 127.20
Tower	119.10 / 128.00
Ground	121.90

NAV Radios

NAVAID	TYPE	FREQUENCY	DESIRED HEADING
PVD	VOR	109.10	320 (FROM)
ORW	VOR	110.0	057 (FROM)
MILTT	NDB	375	Direct
ILQN	ILS	110.30	36 (TO)

The Flight

Use this flight to practice your ATC procedures. Logan International is a busy Class B airport with multiple controllers, and the skies can be crowded. Make sure that you are fully familiar with your comms and navigation plan before you taxi. Set all your radios early, as per your standard preflight checklist (provided in Chapter 2: Aircraft and Checklists). Your first NAV setting can be the PVD VOR, with the OBS on the 320 radial.

You start at a Class C controlled airport, so get your IFR clearance from clearance delivery and contact ground control as advised for further taxi instructions. Follow instructions and comply with each handoff as you complete the taxi and takeoff procedure. You're on an IFR flight plan, so the tower will expect your route of flight to match your clearance. Fly the

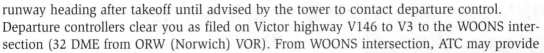

runway heading after takeoff until advised by the tower to contact departure control. Departure controllers clear you as filed on Victor highway V146 to V3 to the WOONS intersection (32 DME from ORW (Norwich) VOR). From WOONS intersection, ATC may provide you with vectors to your destination, but make sure you fly the radial in order to stay inside the established Victor airway.

Boston Approach will guide you into the airport after you've been handed off to them. At WOONS, Approach instructs you to "Turn right heading 080, maintain 4,000 until WINNI (16.9 DME from IBOS), cleared for the ILS 4R at Boston Logan, contact the tower at MILTT." Start your descent and finish setting your radios for the approach. Tune to the ILS frequency in NAV1 and the MILTT outer marker in the ADF. You're looking for a final approach heading of 36, so you have a 44 degree intercept heading. When the localizer comes alive, bank smoothly to a heading of 36. As you cross MILTT (the ADF needle will flip), switch to the tower and get your landing clearance, as shown in Figure 7.4. Once you're down, you'll need to clear the runway as soon as possible and contact ground control for taxi clearance.

If any of the ATC commands are confusing, you can always ask them to repeat. If you're still not sure what they're asking you to do, pause the game and review the ATC Handbook in your online documentation.

Figure 7.4 *On short final at Logan International*

Flight Five: Night Flight Back to Nantucket

Origin: Logan International (KBOS), Boston, MA

Destination: Nantucket Memorial (KACK), Nantucket, MA

Estimated Time En Route: 1 hour

Time of Day: Night

Weather: Broken clouds

Flight Plan: IFR

Route: KBOS BOS V14 GAILS ACK KACK

Altitude: 7,000 feet

Landing: ILS Runway 24

The meeting dragged on through the afternoon, but your boss made it up to you with an excellent meal in Quincy Market. It's evening now, but you and your IFR qualifications are undaunted by night flying!

Radio Information

Logan International (KBOS)

STATION	FREQUENCY
ATIS	135.00
Ground	121.90
Tower	119.10 / 128.00
Departure	133.00

Nantucket Memorial (KACK)

CONTROLLER	FREQUENCY
Approach	126.10
Tower	118.30
Ground	121.70

NAV Radios

NAVAID	TYPE	FREQUENCY	DESIRED HEADING
BOS	VOR	112.70	153 (FROM)
ACK	VOR	116.20	170 (TO)
AC (WAIVS)	NDB	248	Direct
IACK	ILS	109.10	241 (TO)

The Flight

As with the last flight, this is a good chance to practice your ATC interaction at a busy airport, albeit with a departure instead of an arrival. Dial in the BOS VOR in your preflight and go through the full procedure of getting taxi, takeoff, and departure clearances. Don't forget your lights—it's dark out! Use the chase plane view or the "W" key to temporarily peer through your instrument panel if you have a hard time finding your way around the ramp at night.

TIP

You can always check your navigation log screen in the simulator for detailed information about each leg of your trip. When used in conjunction with the radio charts in these walkthroughs, you have everything needed to get to your destination.

Once you're airborne, you'll be looking for the GAILS intersection, which is the same one you used to get to Provincetown and back on previous flights. Establish yourself on Victor 141, the BOS 154 radial (heading "FROM"), as that's the only way you can find GAILS (really just an arbitrary point in space). After you're on the radial, tune to the ACK VOR and look for the intersection with the 169 radial. You can always dial back the OBS to help you anticipate the intersection.

Adjust the OBS until you have a centered course deviation indicator (CDI), and that will tell you how far along you are on the first leg of your trip. Of course, you can also check the DME reading from BOS, which will be 39 nautical miles (NM) from BOS by the time you arrive at GAILS. When you intercept the ACK 170 radial, bank right as in Figure 7.5 and proceed directly.

You'll fight a bit of a headwind on the way back home, but it is essentially the same return you did from Provincetown from here on out, only at night. As long as you trust your instruments and do the same things you did on that flight, you shouldn't have any problems. Upon reaching 12 DME from the ACK (Nantucket) VOR on V141 at the GROGG intersection, Approach issues you a new clearance: "Turn left heading 120, maintain 1,600 until established on the localizer, clear for the ILS 24 approach at Nantucket. Contact the tower on 118.3." Upon contacting Nantucket tower, tower advises you: "Upon reaching 10.5 DME from IACK (the localizer) to turn right to a heading of 195 degrees to intercept the localizer, clear to land!"

Figure 7.5 *Execute a bank turn off the BOS radial for a direct course to the ACK station over Cape Cod Bay.*

Flight Six: Lecture in Northampton

Origin: Nantucket Memorial (KACK), Nantucket, MA

Destination: Northampton Airstrip (7B2), Northampton, MA

Estimated Time En Route: 1 hour, 30 minutes

Time of Day: Noon

Weather: Broken clouds

Flight Plan: IFR

Route: KACK ACK MVY PVD PUT BAF 7B2

Altitude: 6,000 feet

Landing: Visual to runway 32

Your boss is a featured lecturer at a writer's conference in the western Massachusetts city of Northampton. Northampton is home to five colleges and universities, all of which are held in very high regard. Your boss insists on flying into the town's small airstrip, which is the closest field to the campus he will be lecturing at. The Northampton strip is uncontrolled and has no ILS, so you'll be making a Visual Flight Rules (VFR) landing.

Radio Information

Nantucket Memorial (KACK)

STATION	FREQUENCY
Ground	121.70
Tower	118.30
Departure	126.10

Green State (KPVD)

STATION	FREQUENCY
Center	124.850

Northampton (7B2)

STATION	FREQUENCY
Approach	125.65
CTAF	122.70

NAV Radios

NAVAID	TYPE	FREQUENCY	DESIRED HEADING
ACK	VOR	116.20	60 (TO)
MVY	VOR	114.50	299 (TO)
PVD	VOR	109.10	312 (TO)
PUT	VOR	117.40	321 (TO)
BAF	VOR	113.00	301 (TO)
BAF (to 7B2)	VOR	113.00	39 (FROM)

The Flight

The weather is good for flying today, with scattered clouds between 1,500 and 2,500 feet. A light surface wind is nothing to be concerned about, and the visibility is excellent. With Visual Meteorological Conditions (VMC) in effect, you can choose to fly this route under VFR if it suits your fancy. As you can see in Figure 7.6, the Northampton airstrip is fairly spartan and uncontrolled. It is very close to the larger Westover ARB, however, which provides approach and departure control in the local airspace on channel 125.65.

The first half of your flight is identical to your trip to Providence, with a waypoint over the PVD station. Since you'll be on a filed IFR flight plan, you'll automatically be cleared into the airspace when you approach, and you'll be moved on through PUT and BAF. After

Figure 7.6 *Touchdown at the Northampton airstrip*

you reach the BAF station, follow the 39 radial to arrive at the Northampton airstrip. Runway 32 will likely be the easiest runway for a direct approach, although you should check in with Approach control for clearance. Use full flaps on this landing because of the shorter runway length, and set her down nice and slow.

Flight Seven: Home at Last

Origin: Northampton (7B2), Northampton, MA

Destination: Nantucket Memorial (KACK), Nantucket, MA

Estimated Time En Route: 1 hour, 30 minutes

Time of Day: Noon

Weather: Rainstorm

Flight Plan: IFR

Route: 7B2 BAF 146 PUT PVD MVY ACK KACK

Altitude: 7,000 feet

Landing: ILS Runway 24

Over the course of your overnight stay in Northampton, a storm rolled into New England. Despite an attempt to wait it out this morning, the forecast is for continued inclement weather. Winds are gusting to 17 knots, there is turbulence above 6,000 feet, and it is rain-ing fairly heavily. Fortunately, the Cessna 182S is a sturdy bird, so you can look forward to the challenge of the flight home.

Radio Information

Northampton (7B2)

STATION	FREQUENCY
Departure	125.65
CTAF	122.70

Green State (KPVD)

STATION	FREQUENCY
Center	124.850

Nantucket Memorial (KACK)

CONTROLLER	FREQUENCY
Approach	126.10
Tower	118.30
Ground	121.70

NAV Radios

NAVAID	TYPE	FREQUENCY	DESIRED HEADING
BAF	VOR	113.00	217 (TO)
PUT	VOR	117.40	122 (TO)
PVD	VOR	109.10	141 (TO)
MVY	VOR	114.50	133 (TO)
ACK	VOR	116.20	120 (TO)
IACK	ILS	109.10	241 (TO)

The Flight

This trip will test your flight skills in bad weather. Although it's stormy, visibility remains good, so you'll still be able to make use of visual references. Transmit your departure intentions to the CTAF frequency, and then contact departure control at Westover for clearance out of its airspace.

Concentrate on finding the best altitude for your flight. With live ATC, you could request clearance to a higher or lower altitude for safer flying conditions. In this activity, you can simply assume that you have obtained such clearance, though you should refrain from changing altitude too many times. By now you have experience with all the navaids and routes you'll be flying, so all you need to do is get the plane home safely (as seen in Figure 7.7) to complete the activities!

Figure 7.7 *Landing in a rainstorm is challenging, but within the limits of your Cessna's abilities.*

Alaskan Floatplane Pilot

Area: Alaska, U.S.

Aircraft: Cessna 208B Caravan Amphibian

Flights: 6

Difficulty: Medium

This flight series puts you at the controls of the Cessna Caravan, equipped with floats for exciting amphibian operations. You play the part of a charter pilot for Gaia Airlines, based at Merrill Field in Anchorage, Alaska. Your flights will crisscross the south-central region of the state, including several backcountry flights beyond the range of ground-based navigation aids that require GPS (Global Positioning System) use. You'll have to be familiar with water landings and takeoffs, and you'll be flying through varied terrain in a wide range of weather conditions.

Flight One: Chugach Scenic Tour

Origin: Merrill Field (PAMR), Anchorage, AK

Destination: Merrill Field (PAMR), Anchorage, AK

Estimated Time En Route: 30 minutes to 2 hours

Time of Day: Early afternoon

Weather: Clear

Flight Plan: VFR

Route: PAMR PAAQ WP01 WP02 WP03 PAMR

Altitude: 3,500 feet

Landing: VFR (as cleared)

Your first flight with Gaia Airlines is a chartered "flightseeing" trip into Chugach State Park, the third-largest state park in the United States. Its glacier-covered terrain includes the Chugach Range, which begins just east of Anchorage. There, you'll explore the mountains, valleys, and glaciers of the state park from the air and spot some of the moose, mountain goats, Dall sheep, and bears that call the area home.

Radio Information

Merrill Field (PAMR)

STATION	FREQUENCY
ATIS	123.700
Ground	121.700
Tower	126.000
Departure	119.100
Approach	119.100

NAV Radios

NAVAID	TYPE	FREQUENCY	DESIRED HEADING
CMQ	NDB	338.0	–
ANC	VOR/DME	114.30	–
EDF	DME	113.40	–

The Flight

This flight begins on the ramp at Merrill Field in Anchorage, with the engine running. Request taxi clearance for an eastern departure for your VFR journey and take off from the assigned runway following standard ATC procedures. Once airborne, head east until you come to the foothills of the massive Chugach Range. Find the highway shown in Figure 7.8 (look just beneath the foothills) and trace it to the northeast.

Figure 7.8 *Follow the general course in your flight plan, looking for the best views for your passengers.*

As you follow the road, you'll pass three valleys on your right that head into the mountains. The first is the Eagle River Valley, followed by the Peters Creek and Eklutna River Valleys. The latter leads to Eklutna Lake and Bold Airstrip. Beyond these first valley mouths lies the Knik River Valley, which leads to the magnificent Knik Glacier. You may wish to head south from Knik Glacier to Inner Lake George, which offers a landing spot if you want to treat your passengers to a walk on the glacier itself. To the south is Lake George Glacier, and beyond it lies Portage and the waters of the Turnagain Arm.

After you've given your passengers a worthwhile trip, head back to Merrill Field. If the trip has dragged on, return directly by climbing to receive the Anchorage VOR signal. Otherwise, use your chart and the GPS to return via the most scenic route. Request clearance from Approach, and then land and taxi back to the ramp for a successful first flight.

Flight Two: Drop-off at Red Shirt Lake

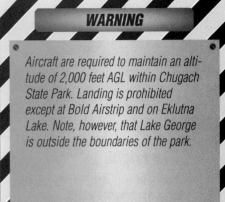

WARNING

Aircraft are required to maintain an altitude of 2,000 feet AGL within Chugach State Park. Landing is prohibited except at Bold Airstrip and on Eklutna Lake. Note, however, that Lake George is outside the boundaries of the park.

Origin: Merrill Field (PAMR), Anchorage, AK

Destination: Merrill Field (PAMR), Anchorage, AK

Estimated Time En Route: 45 minutes

Time of Day: Early afternoon

Weather: Light rain/overcast

Flight Plan: VFR

Route: PAMR BGQ WP01 PAMR

Altitude: 3,500 feet

Landing: VFR (as cleared)

During this activity, you must fly a group of sport fishermen from Merrill Field in Anchorage to Red Shirt Lake. Just 26 NM northwest of Anchorage, Red Shirt Lake is the most popular destination for pike fishermen in the Nancy Lake State Recreation Area. Despite being so close to Anchorage, the only access to many of the lakes in the Susitna River Valley is by floatplane or on foot. Wildlife in the area includes loons, ducks, moose, beavers, and bears.

Radio Information

Merrill Field (PAMR)

STATION	FREQUENCY
ATIS	123.700
Ground	121.700
Tower	126.000
Departure	119.100
Approach	119.100

NAV Radios

NAVAID	TYPE	FREQUENCY	DESIRED HEADING
BCQ	VOR	112.50	326 (TO)
CMQ	NDB	338.0	–
ANC	VOR/DME	114.30	–
EDF	DME	113.40	–

The Flight

Request a northern departure and head northwest after clearing the pattern. The Big Lake VOR (BCQ) provides you with the easiest way to get to the lake. Fly over the station and then move outbound on the Big Lake on a 270-degree radial for six nautical miles. The lake's elevation is 150 feet Mean Sea Level (MSL). Land and drop off your passengers somewhere near the middle of the lake's eastern shore. When you're finished, simply take off and return to Anchorage.

Flight Three: Pickup at Twin Lakes

Origin: Merrill Field (PAMR), Anchorage, AK

Destination: Merrill Field (PAMR), Anchorage, AK

Estimated Time En Route: 1 hour, 30 minutes

Time of Day: Noon

Weather: High clouds

Flight Plan: VFR

Route: PAMR WP01 PAMR

Altitude: 6,500 feet

Landing: VFR (as cleared)

In this flight, you'll fly from your base at Merrill Field to Twin Lakes, where you'll pick up six hikers. Twin Lakes is located at the southwestern end of the Neacola Mountains in Lake Clark National Park and Preserve, approximately 115 miles southwest of Anchorage. The area is representative of all the scenery that Alaska has to offer: majestic glaciers and rivers, imposing mountains and volcanoes, and tundra-covered valleys and hills. Local residents include caribou, moose, bear, wolves, Dall sheep, and plenty of sockeye salmon. The hikers plan to meet you at the east end of the eastern lake at noon. Pick them up and then return to Anchorage.

Radio Information

Merrill Field (PAMR)

STATION	FREQUENCY
ATIS	123.700
Ground	121.700
Tower	126.000
Departure	119.100
Approach	119.100

NAV Radios

NAVAID	TYPE	FREQUENCY	DESIRED HEADING
CMQ	NDB	338.0	–
ANC	VOR/DME	114.30	–
EDF	DME	113.40	–
ILI	NDB	411.0	–

The Flight

As usual, you begin the flight on the ramp with the engine running. Get clearance for a western departure, taxi, and depart Merrill Field. Head southwest on a heading of approximately 140 to take you down Cook Inlet, depicted on the chart for this activity. The course line on your GPS shows the direct route to the lake. Depending on the weather conditions, you are free to choose whichever route you prefer, as long as you are on time to rendezvous with the hikers at noon.

N O T A M
Notice to All Airmen

Within the boundaries of Lake Clark National Park and Preserve, regulations request that you remain at least 2,000 feet above the surface, except when landing or taking off. Other than that, use your discretion to determine the best altitude for this flight.

Twin Lakes is located about 15 miles north of Lake Clark. You can use your GPS to navigate there by proceeding to N60° 37.87' W° 153 55.19'. The lakes are at 2,000 feet MSL in a valley carved by glaciers. If you've been following standard procedure and updating your altimeter settings as ATC relays them, you should be able to execute a smooth landing on the lake (see Figure 7.9). Once you're down, meet the hikers at the east end of the easternmost lake. Load up, do a head count, and take off for home.

When the passengers and their gear are on board, fly back to Anchorage via the route of your choice. The GPS will display the direct route back to the airport, but you may want to

Figure 7.9 *Execute a water landing on the picturesque surface of Twin Lakes.*

alter your track based upon weather conditions or a desire to sightsee. Enter the pattern at Merrill Field as instructed, and then land and taxi to a stop to complete the activity.

Flight Four: Mt. McKinley Scenic Flight

Origin: Merrill Field (PAMR), Anchorage, AK

Destination: Merrill Field (PAMR), Anchorage, AK

Estimated Time En Route: 1 hour, 30 minutes

Time of Day: Noon

Weather: Scattered clouds

Flight Plan: VFR

Route: PAMR TKA WP01 WP02 PAMR

Altitude: 8,500 feet

Landing: VFR (as cleared)

Today's activity is a charter flight for a group of seven tourists interested in a scenic tour of Mt. McKinley. Located about 100 miles northwest of Anchorage, Mt. McKinley sits in the center of Denali National Park. At 20,320 feet, it's the highest peak in North America, so flying over its glacier-covered slopes is an experience your passengers will never forget. After a tour of the mountain, land on Chelatna Lake for lunch before heading back to Anchorage.

Radio Information

Merrill Field (PAMR)

STATION	FREQUENCY
ATIS	123.700
Ground	121.700
Tower	126.000
Departure	119.100
Approach	119.100

NAV Radios

NAVAID	TYPE	FREQUENCY	DESIRED HEADING
TKA	VOR/DME	116.20	329 (TO)
ANC	VOR/DME	114.30	–
EDF	DME	113.40	–

The Flight

Request a northern departure from the airport. After clearing the traffic pattern, point your nose to the northwest. The route you take is up to you. You can use the chart and follow the Susitna River north to Talkeetna, or you can fly directly to the Talkeetna VOR (116.2 TKA). The green course line displayed on the GPS takes you straight to the Talkeetna VOR, and then to the foot of Ruth Glacier, over Lake Chelatna, and finally back to Anchorage. Altitude is at your discretion for this flight, but seeing as Mt. McKinley has a peak (shown in Figure 7.10) over 20,000 feet high, you'll need plenty of it for at least part of your journey!

A good place to start the scenic tour is at the foot of the Ruth Glacier (located on the 310-degree course FROM the Talkeetna VOR, at about 25 DME). Fly up the glacier, taking your time to do some exploring. You will pass through the Great Gorge and into Sheldon Amphitheater (named after pioneer bush pilot Don Sheldon), only six miles or so from the summit. Give your passengers a flight to remember, and when you're done, fly back down Ruth Glacier or cross over to another scenic spot. You're the pilot in command, so it's up to you.

When you're off the mountain, head southwest to Chelatna Lake (1,384 feet MSL). Land and have a floating lunch. Afterwards, head back to Anchorage along the route of your choosing and set down as cleared.

Figure 7.10 *Mt. McKinley is the highest peak in North America.*

Flight Five: Drop-off at Heather Bay

Origin: Merrill Field (PAMR), Anchorage, AK

Destination: Merrill Field (PAMR), Anchorage, AK

Estimated Time En Route: 1 hour, 30 minutes

Time of Day: Early morning

Weather: Rain

Flight Plan: VFR

Route: PAMR HOPR PAWR PAMR

Altitude: 3,500 feet

Landing: VFR (as cleared)

This assignment sees you flying four sea kayakers, their collapsible boats, and their gear to Heather Bay on Prince William Sound. Your passengers plan on spending a week paddling the waters of Prince William Sound, and they'll begin their journey about 100 miles northeast of Anchorage at the foot of Columbia Glacier.

Radio Information

Merrill Field (PAMR)

STATION	FREQUENCY
ATIS	123.700
Ground	121.700
Tower	126.000
Departure	119.100
Approach	119.100

NAV Radios

NAVAID	TYPE	FREQUENCY	DESIRED HEADING
CMQ	NDB	338.0	–
JOH	VOR/DME	116.70	–
ANC	VOR/DME	114.30	–
EDF	DME	113.40	–

The Flight

You begin this flight in the same condition as the other flights in this series, with engines running and ready to go on the ramp. Request an eastern departure and take off as directed by ATC. After clearing the airport pattern, head southeast across the Turnagain Arm. Fly east down Turnagain Arm, through Portage Pass, and out into Prince William Sound. As with the other Alaskan flights, the exact route you take is up to you. In this flight, the GPS course leads from Merrill Field to Portage, then east past the north side of Storey Island, north over Glacier Island to Heather Bay, and straight back to Merrill Field.

> **⟳ N O T A M ⟳**
> **Notice to All Airmen**
>
> Remember to reset your altimeter (click the knob or press "B") to the new settings as you get them from ATC.

Heather Bay is located 20 miles southwest of Valdez at the foot of the Columbia Glacier at N61° 01.54', W146° 57.52'. The bay is part of Prince William Sound, so it's at sea level. Drop the passengers off anywhere along the shore. After your passengers and their gear are out, head back to Anchorage via the route of your choice. The green course line on the GPS is the direct route over the mountains, but you might not be able to take this if the clouds are low (see the minimum VFR visibility regulations in Chapter 3: Navigation). When you get back to Merrill Field, land as directed and chalk up another successful flight into the bush!

Flight Six: Drop-off at Kenai

Origin: Merrill Field (PAMR), Anchorage, AK

Destination: Kenai Municipal Airport (PAEN), AK

Estimated Time En Route: 45 minutes

Time of Day: Afternoon

Weather: Low clouds/poor visibility

Flight Plan: VFR

Route: PAMR PAEN

Altitude: 4,500 feet

Landing: VFR (as cleared)

The last flight in the Alaskan Floatplane series is a drop-off in Kenai, southwest of your home base at Merrill. A team of oil executives is flying out of Anchorage to visit installations on the Kenai Peninsula, and you're assigned to get them there.

Radio Information

Merrill Field (PAMR)

STATION	FREQUENCY
ATIS	123.700
Ground	121.700
Tower	126.000
Departure	119.100

Kenai Municipal Airport (PAEN)

STATION	FREQUENCY
Tower	121.300
Ground	121.900

NAV Radios

NAVAID	TYPE	FREQUENCY	DESIRED HEADING
ENA	VOR/DME	117.60	202
ANC	VOR/DME	114.30	–
IENA	ILS (19R)	108.90	187

The Flight

Weather is marginal for a VFR flight this afternoon, with low clouds and poor visibility. However, VMC prevail, so you deem it safe to fly. Request permission to taxi from the ramp for a western departure. Clear the pattern and head southwest across Cook Inlet. You can use the chart and follow the eastern shore of Cook Inlet, or you can just fly directly to the Kenai (ENA) VOR at 117.60. Naturally, the GPS displays the direct route.

Kenai Airport is located just south of the VOR at 97 feet MSL (refer to the chart above for specifics, or see your online Flight Planner). Enter the pattern as instructed, land, and taxi to the parking area to finish your exploits in Alaska.

Desert Adventure

Area: Southwestern U.S.

Aircraft: Cessna 208B Caravan Amphibian

Flights: 5

Difficulty: Medium

There's a lot more to the desert than just sun and sand. In this breathtaking series of flights, you'll rent a Cessna 182S at North Las Vegas Airport and embark on a two-day aerial adventure over the mountains, deserts, and canyons of the American Southwest. Scenic highlights include Hoover Dam, the Grand Canyon, Lake Mead, and flying over the City of Lights, Las Vegas. VFR flight plans allow you to chase rainbows on a whim and relax the difficulty level somewhat.

Flight One: North Las Vegas to Pearce Ferry

Origin: North Las Vegas Airport (KVGT), Las Vegas, Nevada

Destination: Pearce Ferry Airport (L25), Meadview, Arizona

Estimated Time En Route: 1 hour

Time of Day: Early morning

Weather: High clouds

Flight Plan: VFR

Route: KVGT (WP01–WP05) L25

Altitude: 5,500 feet

Landing: Active runway/uncontrolled

N O T A M
Notice to All Airmen

To assist you in navigating the complex airspace around Las Vegas and the Grand Canyon, there is a flight plan associated with this activity. Thus, in addition to the charts, you can use the GPS and the Navigation Log to help you navigate.

This first flight in the Desert Adventure series takes you southeast from North Las Vegas over Lake Mead and Hoover Dam. You will then fly east along the Nevada–Arizona border and up Lake Mead to Pearce Ferry.

Yesterday morning you flew into Las Vegas' McCarran International Airport on a commercial airliner, and then took a taxi to North Las Vegas Airport, one of the city's smaller general aviation airports. You spent the afternoon getting checked out in the Cessna 182S that you'll be renting for the next four days (see Figure 7.11).

Figure 7.11 *A Cessna 182S over the infamous Las Vegas Strip*

This morning you awoke with anticipation long before sunrise. After a quick breakfast in the hotel restaurant, you headed out to the airport in the dark. It's always a good idea to get an early start in the desert to avoid the midday wind, turbulence, and increased density altitude caused by the hot sun. You preflight the plane, and by 5:30 in the morning, you're ready to go.

Radio Information

North Las Vegas Airport (KVGT)

STATION	FREQUENCY
ATIS	118.050
Delivery	124.000
Ground	121.700
Tower	125.700
Departure	133.950

Pearce Ferry Airport (L25)

STATION	FREQUENCY
CTAF	122.900

NAV Radios

NAVAID	TYPE	FREQUENCY	DESIRED HEADING
LAS	VOR/DME	116.90	–

The Flight

The flight begins with the airplane parked on the ramp at North Las Vegas Airport. The engine is running. When you're ready to go, call up ground control and request permission to taxi for a south departure. Then taxi to the assigned runway. To make taxiing easier, you can press "S" to cycle to an external view, or you can request progressive taxi instructions.

Take off from North Las Vegas Airport, head southwest to intercept the green course line displayed on the GPS, and climb to 4,000 feet MSL. This route, called the "Showboat Departure," will take you southwest a few miles and then east past the hotels and casinos of the infamous Las Vegas Strip. You'll see McCarran International Airport (KLAS) to the south and Nellis Air Force Base (KLSV) to the north.

The route then takes you east out of the city to Wash Marina at the west end of Lake Mead. One of the largest artificial lakes in the world, Lake Mead was formed in 1935 when Hoover Dam was constructed on the Colorado River. Lake Mead is a National Recreation Area, so you should stay at least 2,000 feet above the terrain at all times. Follow the GPS course line along the western shore of the lake southeast to Hoover Dam (see Figure 7.12).

Make some circles to take a good look at the dam, and then follow the GPS course line northeast along the lake's southern shore and climb to your final cruising altitude of 5,500 feet MSL. Use the autopilot to maintain altitude if you want. The lake narrows just to the south of the Black Mountains and then widens out again, with a long arm reaching to

Figure 7.12 *The awe-inspiring Hoover Dam at Lake Mead*

the north. Eventually, you might be able to make out Temple Bar Airport (U30) off your right wing (you'll see it on the GPS).

NOTAM
Notice to All Airmen
Remember to announce your approach and landing progress on the Common Traffic Advisory Frequency (CTAF) at Pearce Ferry, which is an uncontrolled airport.

About 15 miles past Temple Bar, you'll arrive over Pearce Ferry Airport (L25), a dirt strip on a plateau a few miles from the western mouth of the Grand Canyon. Named after the ferry that used to operate across the lake, Pearce Ferry now serves as the starting point for rafting trips down the Colorado River through the canyon. Since the airstrip is in the Lake Mead National Recreation Area, regulations request that you stay within three miles of the airport as you descend for landing. Land and taxi to the parking area of your choice to successfully complete your first desert flight.

Flight Two: Pearce Ferry to Grand Canyon National Park

Origin: Pearce Ferry Airport (L25), Meadview, Arizona

Destination: Grand Canyon National Park Airport (KGCN), Grand Canyon, Arizona

Estimated Time En Route: 1 hour, 30 minutes

Time of Day: Morning

Weather: High clouds/increasing winds

Flight Plan: VFR

Route: L25 (WP01–WP10) KGCN

Altitude: 9,500 feet

Landing: VFR (as cleared)

After a snack and a short hike in the desert surrounding the Pearce Ferry Airport, you're ready to go. You give the plane a quick preflight inspection and climb inside. This leg will take you from Pearce Ferry east over the Grand Canyon to Grand Canyon National Park Airport. The route cuts back and forth across the canyon, and will give you plenty of good views of the Colorado River and some side canyons.

Flying the Grand Canyon

In the good old days, aircraft could actually fly down into the Grand Canyon. But when commercial sightseeing traffic began to increase in the 1980s, the FAA decided to regulate the airspace over the canyon. The result is a series of "Flight-Free Zones," where aircraft are not permitted, and highly regulated airspace everywhere else. It's a complex system, but it ensures that everyone who wants to see the canyon from the air can do so, while mini-mizing the impact on the wildlife and visitors down below.

In the real world, pilots must monitor specific radio frequencies in each zone and give frequent location reports to other aircraft in the area. In Flight Simulator 2002, *just follow the green course line displayed on the GPS. It will take you between many of the real-world reporting points and will keep you out of the Flight-Free Zones. For an even more realistic flight, maintain the altitudes mentioned in the following sections. You'll be amazed at how much there is to see, even with all of the airspace regulations.*

Radio Information

Pearce Ferry Airport (L25)

STATION	FREQUENCY
CTAF	122.900

Grand Canyon National Park Airport (KGCN)

STATION	FREQUENCY
Center	124.200
Tower	119.000
Ground	121.900

NAV Radios

NAVAID	TYPE	FREQUENCY	DESIRED HEADING
PGS	VOR/DME	112.00	–
GCN	VOR/DME	113.10	68
IGCN	ILS (3)	108.90	27

The Flight

Today's flight begins with your Cessna 182S parked on the ramp at Pearce Ferry Airport (probably at a different location than where you left it) with its engine running. When you're ready to go, announce your intentions and then taxi to the assigned runway. To make taxiing easier, press "S" to cycle to an external view.

WARNING

Remember that since the airport is in the Lake Mead National Recreation Area, the regulations require you to stay within three miles of the airport until you're at least 2,000 feet above ground level.

The ceiling of the Grand Canyon Special Flight Rules area that you're about to enter ("Pearce Ferry Sector") is 7,999 feet MSL. So you need to be above that altitude before heading east. Take off and circle the airport as you climb, staying within the designated three-mile radius. When you are above 5,000 feet MSL, head northwest over the lake as you continue climbing. When you're at least 8,000 feet MSL, head east to intercept the GPS course line leading northeast from the airport to the canyon.

As you proceed along the route, climb to your initial cruising altitude of 9,500 feet MSL and continue following the GPS course line. When flying over the canyon, stay to the right. Use the GPS line as just a general guide—feel free to deviate a bit and do some exploring, as shown in Figure 7.13.

About an hour into the flight, when you reach the northernmost waypoint along the route (WP08), climb to 11,500 feet MSL so you'll be at the proper altitude when you cross into the next sector. From this point, the course follows Havasu Creek southeast away from the Colorado River to Havatagvitch Canyon and South Supai Canyon, and then east toward Grand Canyon National Park Airport (KGCN). After passing waypoint WP10 and turning east, start descending to pattern altitude (7,600 feet MSL) and contact the tower. Enter the pattern as instructed, land, and then taxi to a good parking spot.

Figure 7.13 *The wonder and beauty of the Grand Canyon speaks for itself.*

Flight Three: Grand Canyon Sunset Flight

Origin: Grand Canyon National Park Airport (KGCN), Grand Canyon, Arizona

Destination: Grand Canyon National Park Airport (KGCN), Grand Canyon, Arizona

Estimated Time En Route: 45 minutes

Time of Day: Early evening

Weather: High clouds/gusting afternoon desert winds

Flight Plan: VFR

Route: KGCN (WP01–WP08) KGCN

Altitude: 11,500 feet

Landing: VFR (as cleared)

After a fun day at the south rim of the Grand Canyon, you return to the airport for a flight over the beautiful area at sunset. The green course line on the GPS follows a route similar to one that many tour operators use, so it will give you a good look at the scenery while keeping you out of the Flight-Free Zones. Follow the course line and the altitudes noted in the following sections, and your flight should be very close to what you can experience in the real world. Feel free, however, to deviate a bit and do some exploring.

Radio Information

Grand Canyon National Park Airport (KGCN)

STATION	FREQUENCY
ATIS	124.300
Ground	121.900
Tower	119.000
Center	124.200

NAV Radios

NAVAID	TYPE	FREQUENCY	DESIRED HEADING
GCN	VOR/DME	113.10	–
IGCN	ILS (3)	108.90	27

The Flight

Request permission to taxi for an eastern departure, and then taxi to the assigned runway. Take off, and when you're clear of the traffic pattern, head east to intercept the green course line on the GPS. Climb to 11,500 feet MSL (the altitude for northbound traffic through the corridors). Remember to lean the fuel mixture above 3,000 feet if you're using full realism to get the best performance out of the engine. Consider using the autopilot to help maintain altitude. This will allow you to divert some of your attention to the great views of the canyon off your left wing.

After about 15 miles, you'll reach checkpoint "Zuni Alpha" (WP02 on the GPS). Follow the course line north through the Zuni Point Corridor, and then travel east over the Little Colorado River Canyon. Explore this side canyon, and then follow the GPS course line west. As the Grand Canyon's north rim is 1,000 feet higher than the south rim, don't be surprised when you find yourself closer to the ground. Continue west, descend to 10,500 feet MSL (the regulated altitude for southbound traffic through the corridors), and follow the course line south down Dragon Corridor. Over "The Ranch" (a private airstrip), the course turns east back toward Grand Canyon Airport. After turning east, start descending to pattern altitude (7,600 feet MSL) and contact the tower. Enter the pattern as instructed and land to end your flight.

Flight Four: Grand Canyon National Park to Echo Bay

Origin: Grand Canyon National Park Airport (KGCN), Grand Canyon, Arizona

Destination: Echo Bay Airport (0L9), Overton, Nevada

Estimated Time En Route: 1 hour, 30 minutes

Time of Day: Morning

Weather: High clouds

Flight Plan: VFR

Route: KGCN GCN PGS U30 0L9

Altitude: 10,500 feet

Landing: Active runway/uncontrolled

After a restful night in Grand Canyon Village, you arrive at the airport at 7:30 A.M. The line crew fueled the plane as you requested, so just do a preflight inspection and climb inside. For this flight, you'll use basic VOR navigation to fly from Grand Canyon National Park Airport southwest to the Peach Springs VOR, and then northwest over Temple Bar Airport and Lake Mead to Echo Bay. To help you navigate, use the chart (above) and the Navigation Log (on the Flights menu, choose Navigation Log). If you want extra situational awareness, use the GPS.

Radio Information

Grand Canyon National Park Airport (KGCN)

STATION	FREQUENCY
ATIS	124.300
Ground	121.900
Tower	119.000
Center	124.200

Echo Bay Airport (0L9)

STATION	FREQUENCY
CTAF	122.800

NAV Radios

NAVAID	TYPE	FREQUENCY	DESIRED HEADING
GCN	VOR/DME	113.10	13
PGS	VOR	112.00	240 (TO)
			288 (FROM)
LAS	VOR/DME	116.90	–

The Flight

When you're ready to go, call up ground control and request permission to taxi for a west departure. As you clear the traffic pattern after takeoff (see Figure 7.14), start climbing to your initial cruising altitude of 10,500 feet MSL and head southwest. Intercept the 239-degree course FROM the Grand Canyon VOR (GCN 113.10).

Figure 7.14 Beginning the southward turn after clearing the Grand Canyon Airport traffic pattern

After you've flown about 35 miles from the Grand Canyon VOR, tune in the Peach Springs VOR (PGS 112.0) and track the 238-degree course TO the VOR. Crossing the Peach Springs VOR, start descending to 8,500 feet MSL. Intercept and track the 288-degree course FROM the VOR. Upon reaching Temple Bar Airport (U30) at the south end of Lake Mead, fly on a heading of 325 degrees for 18.5 miles up Overton Arm to Echo Bay (0L9). Begin your descent while still over the lake. Enter the traffic pattern at Echo Bay (airport elevation 1,535 feet MSL), land, and taxi to the parking area to complete the activity.

Flight Five: Echo Bay to North Las Vegas

Origin: Echo Bay Airport (0L9), Overton, Nevada

Destination: North Las Vegas Airport (KVGT), Las Vegas, Nevada

Estimated Time En Route: 1 hour, 30 minutes

Time of Day: Evening

Weather: High clouds

Flight Plan: VFR

Route: 0L9 (WP01–WP04) KVGT

Altitude: 4,500 feet

Landing: Active runway/uncontrolled

All things come to an end, and so too must your desert adventure. Having spent a fun day on the water, it's time to head back to Las Vegas to catch your commercial flight home. This short flight will take you down Lake Mead's Overton Arm to Middle Point, and then west over the lake to Wash Marina. From there, you'll follow the "Showboat 1 Arrival" procedure back to North Las Vegas Airport.

Radio Information

Echo Bay Airport (0L9)

STATION	FREQUENCY
CTAF	122.800

North Las Vegas Airport (KVGT)

STATION	FREQUENCY
Approach	124.950
Tower	125.700
Ground	121.700

NAV Radios

NAVAID	TYPE	FREQUENCY	DESIRED HEADING
LAS	VOR/DME	116.90	247

The Flight

Announce an eastern departure at Echo Bay and take off when it is safe to do so. Proceed east to the shoreline and follow the western shore of Lake Mead south to Middle Point. Climb to your cruising altitude of 4,500 feet MSL. Trace the shoreline around Middle Point to the west. You'll pass between the Black Mountains to the north and Mt. Wilson to the south.

Tune in the Las Vegas VOR (LAS 116.9) and track the 246-degree course TO the VOR. Approaching Wash Marina (about 14 NM from the LAS VOR), descend to 3,000 feet MSL. You'll now fly the Showboat 1 Arrival, a VFR transition route that takes pilots headed for

WARNING

Remember, Lake Mead is a National Recreation Area, so the regulations require you to stay 2,000 feet above ground level at all times.

North Las Vegas through the Las Vegas Class B airspace. The track is fully programmed into your GPS, so don't worry if you don't have an arrival chart.

Follow the green GPS course line west to the Showboat Hotel and then northwest to the North Las Vegas Airport (see Figure 7.15). You'll see the lights of The Strip off your left wing and McCarran International Airport further to the south. Contact North Las Vegas tower, enter the pattern as instructed, land, and taxi to parking. Congratulations on completing your Southwestern flying vacation! To extend the adventure by one more flight, create a new activity and employ a commercial airliner to take you to your real home from Las Vegas' McCarran International Airport.

Figure 7.15 *The Showboat 1 Arrival is appropriately named after the landmark it passes over.*

Hawaiian Vacation

Area: Hawaii, U.S.

Aircraft: Cessna 172SP Skyhawk

Flights: 7

Difficulty: Easy

Take a private pilot's dream vacation! Rent a Cessna 172SP in Honolulu and take off on a four-day exploration of the Hawaiian Islands. There's nothing quite like viewing the unspoiled beauty of Hawaii's beaches, volcanoes, and canyons from the air. Navigating between the islands (sometimes out of sight of land) adds to both the challenge and the thrill.

Hawaiian Cruising Altitudes

Because airplanes fly so low over the waters of the Hawaiian Islands, Hawaii has its own VFR cruising altitudes below 3,000 feet. For a more realistic experience when flying eastbound, fly at 500, 1,500, or 2,500 feet MSL. When flying westbound, fly at 1,000, 2,000, or 3,000 feet MSL. Remember to reset your altimeter (click the knob or press "B") to new settings as soon as you get them from ATC.

Flight One: Around Oahu

Origin: Honolulu International Airport (PHNL), Oahu, Hawaii

Destination: Honolulu International Airport (PHNL), Oahu, Hawaii

Estimated Time En Route: 1 hour

Time of Day: Afternoon

Weather: Clear

Flight Plan: VFR

Route: PHNL PHNL

Altitude: Discretionary

Landing: VFR (as cleared)

N O T A M
Notice to All Airmen

Pilots flying in the Hawaiian Islands typically utilize the "Island Reporting Service." They file a special flight plan and use the radio to give frequent position reports to the Flight Service Station. This increases their chances of being rescued quickly in the event of engine trouble while flying over water. *Flight Simulator 2002*'s ATC feature lacks an Island Reporting Service, but you can request Flight Following.

After renting a Cessna 172SP Skyhawk in Honolulu, you're off for a four-day flying adventure around the island paradise of Hawaii. Today, there's only time to explore Oahu, but it'll still be a good introduction to flying in the region. This is purely a recreational excursion flight, so you've got no flight plan—just explore Oahu, observing all VFR regulations as you go. Use the sectional chart above along with VORs to track your progress. Rely upon your GPS for general positional awareness.

Radio Information

Honolulu International Airport (PHNL)

STATION	FREQUENCY
ATIS	127.900
Delivery	121.400
Ground	121.900
Tower	118.100
Departure	118.300
Approach	120.900

NAV Radios

NAVAID	TYPE	FREQUENCY	DESIRED HEADING
HNL	VOR/DME	114.80	–
CKH	VOR/DME	113.90	–
NGF	NDB	265.0	–

The Flight

Your excursion to the South Pacific begins with the airplane parked on the ramp at Honolulu International Airport. The engine is running. When you're ready to go, call ground control and request permission to taxi for an eastern departure. Then taxi to the assigned runway for takeoff. After you are safely aloft, head east past downtown Honolulu toward Punchbowl and Diamond Head craters.

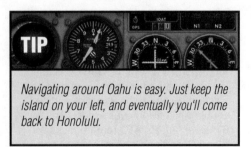

TIP

Navigating around Oahu is easy. Just keep the island on your left, and eventually you'll come back to Honolulu.

Follow the base of the Koolau Mountains to Makapuu Point at the island's eastern end, and then turn northwest. You'll soon fly over Waimanalo Beach and Kailua. If you're above 2,500 feet MSL as you approach Kaneohe Bay Airport (PHNG), request permission to pass through its Class D airspace. Continue northwest along the north side of the island, flying over some of the world's most famous surfing beaches (see Figure 7.16). From Kahuku Point, head south over Dillingham Airfield (PHDH), an uncontrolled airport near Kaena Point. For some extra fun, make a touch-and-go landing, or set down for a while and have a look around.

Figure 7.16 *The beaches of Oahu are wonderful places, whether you're on the ground or in the air.*

As you head southeast past Waianae and Nanakuli, request a transition through the Kalaeloa Airport (PHJR) Class D airspace. Then head for Pearl Harbor. Request permission to transition through the Honolulu International Class B airspace and explore Pearl Harbor, site of the infamous Japanese sneak attack on the United States in 1941.

After you've taken in your fill of the harbor sites and memorials, contact Honolulu Tower and request landing clearance. The airport is just south of the harbor, so you can use the HNL VOR. Head to the airport, land on the assigned runway, and taxi to the parking area of your choice.

Flight Two: Honolulu to Kahului

Origin: Honolulu International Airport (PHNL), Oahu, Hawaii

Destination: Kahului Airport (PHOG), Maui, Hawaii

Estimated Time En Route: 2–3 hours

Time of Day: Morning

Weather: Clear

Flight Plan: VFR

Route: PHNL PHOG

Altitude: Discretionary

Landing: VFR (as cleared)

Today's flight will take you east from Honolulu to the north shore of Molokai, around that island, south to Lanai, and then northeast to Maui.

Radio Information

Honolulu International Airport (PHNL)

STATION	FREQUENCY
ATIS	127.900
Delivery	121.400
Ground	121.900
Tower	118.100
Departure	118.300

Kahului Airport (PHOG)

STATION	FREQUENCY
Approach	119.500
Tower	118.700
Ground	121.900

NAV Radios

NAVAID	TYPE	FREQUENCY	DESIRED HEADING
HNL	VOR/DME	114.80	–
MKK	VOR/DME	116.1	–
LNY	VOR/DME	117.70	107 (FROM)
OGG	VOR/DME	115.10	–

The Flight

With your engine running, everything is set for a taxi onto the ramp. Request permission to taxi for an east departure and take off. Head east past downtown Honolulu, toward Punchbowl and Diamond Head craters en route to Koko Head. From Koko Head, continue

out over the open water to the east. Tune in the Molokai VOR (116.1 MKK) and fly directly to it (on a course of about 093 degrees).

The Molokai VOR will bring you straight into Molokai itself. Spend some time exploring, especially around the spectacular cliffs and valleys along the island's northern coast (see Figure 7.17). After sightseeing a bit, tune in the Lanai VOR (117.7 LNY) and fly directly to it. Lanai once

TIP

For maximum engine performance and efficiency, remember to lean the mixture if you fly higher than 3,000 feet MSL.

boasted the world's largest pineapple fields. Now, it's tourism that attracts visitors to this little island. Take a look around, and if you need a break, land at Lanai Airport (PHNY).

Figure 7.17 *The island of Molokai boasts a spectacular northern coastline.*

When you're finished sightseeing over Lanai, track the 107-degree course from the VOR. You'll soon arrive over the northern end of Kahoolawe, a desolate island once used as a prison. Turn north and fly over a tiny, crescent-shaped island called Molokini. Then continue a few miles north to Maui, one of the most popular destinations in Hawaii. The island was formed by two volcanoes, and the remnants of their power are still visible in the heights. To the west are the West Maui Mountains, while Haleakala Volcano lies to the east, and between them is Maui's Central Valley. Take some time and explore the western end of the island and the valley before setting down at Kahului Airport to complete the flight.

Flight Three: Kahului to Hana

Origin: Kahului Airport (PHOG), Maui, Hawaii

Destination: Hana Airport (PHHN), Maui, Hawaii

Estimated Time En Route: 30–45 minutes

Time of Day: Noon

Weather: Clear

Flight Plan: VFR

Route: PHOG PHHN

Altitude: Discretionary

Landing: Active runway/uncontrolled

After eating lunch and refueling, you climb back into the plane. In this flight, you'll head for Hana on an overnight excursion. Along the way, you can explore Haleakala Volcano, which looms more than 10,000 feet above the sea.

Radio Information

Kahului Airport (PHOG)

STATION	FREQUENCY
ATIS	128.600
Delivery	120.600
Ground	121.900
Tower	118.700
Departure	119.500

Hana Airport (PHHN)

STATION	FREQUENCY
CTAF	122.900

NAV Radios

NAVAID	TYPE	FREQUENCY	DESIRED HEADING
OGG	VOR/DME	115.10	—

The Flight

Request permission to taxi for an east departure and take off heading east along the shoreline. Follow the Hana Highway past the Central Valley. Off your right wing, you'll see Haleakala Volcano rising into the sky (see Figure 7.18). Explore the mountain and the eastern side of the island. Pioneering aviator Charles Lindbergh spent the last years of his life in northeastern Maui and is buried near a small church there—see if you can find it!

Figure 7.18 *The mighty Haleakala Volcano dominates the landscape of the island it created.*

Explore the many and varied sights of Maui. When you're done adventuring for the day, fly to Hana Airport (PHHN) for a landing. There is no control tower, so announce your intentions on the CTAF, and then land and taxi to the parking area of your choice.

Flight Four: Hana to Kona

Origin: Hana Airport (PHHN), Maui, Hawaii

Destination: Kona International Airport (PHKO), Big Island, Hawaii

Estimated Time En Route: 2–3 hours

Time of Day: Morning

Weather: Clear

Flight Plan: VFR

Route: PHHN PHKO

Altitude: Discretionary

Landing: VFR (as cleared)

It's another beautiful morning in the Hawaiian Islands. Today's journey is to Hawaii (also known as "The Big Island"). You'll make a flight over water from Maui to Hawaii's Upolu Point, and then spend the afternoon flying over the island's massive volcanoes. The day will be wrapped up at Kona International Airport.

Radio Information

Hana Airport (PHHN)

STATION	FREQUENCY
CTAF	122.900

Kona International Airport (PHKO)

STATION	FREQUENCY
Tower	120.300

NAV Radios

NAVAID	TYPE	FREQUENCY	DESIRED HEADING
UPP	VOR/DME	112.30	153
MUE	VOR/DME	113.30	–
IAI	VOR/DME	115.70	–

The Flight

Announce your intent to depart to the south and take off from Hana. Tune your NAV radio to the Upolu Point (UPP) VOR and fly a direct course (which should be a heading of about 155 degrees). You'll soon leave Maui and head out over the water. The island of Hawaii will appear on the horizon within minutes. As you approach the shoreline, you'll see Upolu Airport (PHUP).

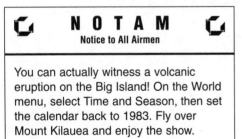

N O T A M

Notice to All Airmen

You can actually witness a volcanic eruption on the Big Island! On the World menu, select Time and Season, then set the calendar back to 1983. Fly over Mount Kilauea and enjoy the show.

From here, the route to take is up to you. Scenic highlights on Hawaii include the Waipo Valley (along the coast, north of Waimea–Kohala Airport), the beaches of the Kona coast (on the west side of the island), Kealakekua Bay (south of Kona International Airport), and of course the volcanoes. Mauna Kea begins 30,000 feet below the ocean's surface and is therefore really the world's tallest mountain. Mauna Loa is an enormous volcano with rift zones that reach all the way to Hilo. Shown in Figure 7.19, Mount Kilauea is the island's most active volcano, regularly erupting since 1983.

Figure 7.19 *Kilauea's eruptions are a unique marvel to behold in* Flight Simulator 2002.

When you've finished sightseeing on the Big Island, head to Kona International Airport (PHKO) to the west. Land and taxi to the parking area of your choice to complete this flight.

Flight Five: Kona to Lihue

Origin: Kona International Airport (PHKO), Big Island, Hawaii

Destination: Lihue Airport (PHLI), Kauai, Hawaii

Estimated Time En Route: 2 hours, 30 minutes

Time of Day: Morning

Weather: Clear

Flight Plan: VFR

Route: PHKO PHLI

Altitude: Discretionary

Landing: VFR (as cleared)

On this flight, you'll make a long journey west to Kauai, past all the islands visited so far. Kauai is often referred to as the "Garden Isle," and many people consider it to be the most beautiful of the Hawaiian chain. The flight includes a crossing over water from Oahu. As it involves a trip of more than 60 miles, you will likely lose sight of land.

Radio Information

Kona International Airport (PHKO)

STATION	FREQUENCY
ATIS	127.400
Delivery	121.900
Tower	120.300

Lihue Airport (PHLI)

STATION	FREQUENCY
Tower	118.900
Ground	121.900

NAV Radios

NAVAID	TYPE	FREQUENCY	DESIRED HEADING
UPP	VOR/DME	112.30	12 (TO)
OGG	VOR/DME	115.10	311 (TO)
MKK	VOR/DME	116.10	277 (TO)
CKH	VOR/DME	113.90	273 (TO)
HNL	VOR/DME	114.80	270 (TO)
LIH	VOR/DME	113.50	286 (TO)

The Flight

Request a departure to the north and take off when cleared by ATC. When airborne, fly north to Upolu Point. If you need help getting there, tune in the Upolu Point (UPP) VOR and fly to it. To get to Kauai, you first have to get back to Honolulu. The route you take is up to you (see Figure 7.20), though for safety reasons you should try to stay within gliding distance of land as often as possible. The higher you are, the further you can glide should there be engine problems. If you fly above 3,000 feet MSL, you can use a normal VFR cruising altitude (an even altitude plus 500 feet, since you're heading west), such as 6,500 feet MSL. If you choose to stay low, use a westbound Hawaiian cruising altitude: 1,000, 2,000, or 3,000 feet MSL.

Keep an eye on the charts while navigating along your route. You may find it easiest to generate a flight plan with the Flight Planner if you don't like the idea of on-the-fly naviga-

Figure 7.20 *You'll be out of sight of land for a portion of this flight, so track your position closely.*

tion. Use GPS routing to generate a direct track, and then drag and drop your course line to the following route: PHKO UPP OGG MKK CKH HNL PHLI. The navigation log in the briefing above details the entire route. If you follow it step by step, it will take you all the way to Lihue. Note that you can deviate from the plan at any time and simply fly direct to the next VOR when you're ready to resume your trip.

When heading west from Oahu, tune in the Lihue VOR (113.5 LIH) and track to it. Get clearance, land, and taxi to the parking area of your choice. You'll have a chance to explore the island's breathtaking natural beauty on your next flight.

Flight Six: Kauai Tour

Origin: Lihue Airport (PHLI), Kauai, Hawaii

Destination: Lihue Airport (PHLI), Kauai, Hawaii

Estimated Time En Route: 1 hour

Time of Day: Morning

Weather: Clear

Flight Plan: VFR

Route: PHNL PHNL

Altitude: Discretionary

Landing: VFR (as cleared)

After a delicious breakfast, you head out to the airport, excited to explore Kauai from the air. If there is one island in the Hawaiian chain that's a true tropical paradise, it's this one. Your flight plan is open as always, with a roundtrip planned from Lihue Airport.

Radio Information

Lihue Airport (PHLI)

STATION	FREQUENCY
Ground	121.900
Tower	118.900

NAV Radios

NAVAID	TYPE	FREQUENCY	DESIRED HEADING
LIH	VOR/DME	113.50	–
NBS	DME	112.60	–
SOK	VOR/DME	115.40	–

The Flight

There's no wrong way to fly around Kauai: all sides of the island have wondrous sights to offer, and the interior contains some of the most impressive scenery in the hemisphere. There are a few places you'll probably want to go, however. Just offshore of Waimea, where the Waimea River flows into the ocean, is the spot where the first Westerners to discover Hawaii (led by British naval captain James Cook) anchored their ships in 1778. If you follow the Waimea River north, it will lead to the mighty Waimea Canyon (see Figure 7.21), which is called "The Grand Canyon of the Pacific." This nickname was coined by Mark Twain, in part because of the canyon's impressive depth of 3,600 feet.

From the top of Waimea Canyon, a ridgeline drops straight off to the Na Pali Coast, along the western shore of the island just south of Haena. There you'll find deserted beaches and stunning cliffs so beautiful that you've got to see them to believe them. Five-thousand-foot Mt. Waialeale, in the center of the island, is one of the wettest places on earth, with an annual rainfall of over 450 inches! The peak, called Kawaikini, is almost always hidden by clouds. This rainfall and its subsequent runoff created the impressive Waimea Canyon.

When you've used up most of your fuel (since you can never be "done" taking in Kauai's beautiful scenery), head back to Lihue for a landing to finish the flight. Your next activity will be in the direction of home, so savor the scenic moments while they last.

Figure 7.21 *Mark Twain nicknamed Waimea Canyon "The Grand Canyon of the Pacific" after seeing the chasm's red, green, and purple colors.*

Flight Seven: Lihue to Honolulu

Origin: Lihue Airport (PHLI), Kauai, Hawaii

Destination: Honolulu International Airport (PHNL), Oahu, Hawaii

Estimated Time En Route: 1 hour

Time of Day: Afternoon

Weather: Clear

Flight Plan: VFR

Route: PHLI PHNL

Altitude: Discretionary

Landing: VFR (as cleared)

All vacations must unfortunately come to an end, so it's time to head back to Honolulu and return the Cessna 172SP. You get some fuel, give the airplane a careful preflight inspection, and climb inside for a final spin above the islands.

Radio Information

Lihue Airport (PHLI)

STATION	FREQUENCY
Ground	121.900
Tower	118.900

Honolulu International Airport (PHNL)

STATION	FREQUENCY
Approach	120.900
Tower	118.100
Ground	121.900

NAV Radios

NAVAID	TYPE	FREQUENCY	DESIRED HEADING
LIH	VOR/DME	113.50	110 (FROM)
HNL	VOR/DME	114.80	–

The Flight

This flight is fairly straightforward. Take off from Lihue with an eastern departure clearance. Tune in the Lihue (LIH) VOR and track the 110-degree course from the VOR toward Oahu. On the leg that takes you over the water, grab some altitude to about 10,000 feet to extend your glide range in case of engine failure. When you reach the southwest corner of Oahu, tune in the Honolulu (HNL) VOR and proceed directly to Honolulu International Airport (PHNL). Land and taxi to the parking area to complete your Hawaiian vacation!

Scenic Wonders

Area: Worldwide

Aircraft: Variable

Flights: 12

Difficulty: Easy

The series of Scenic Wonders flights puts you in the cockpit of various airplanes over some of the most spectacular natural wonders that *Flight Simulator 2002* has to offer. Each scenario begins with the airplane already in the air, so there's no takeoff clearance to worry about. These are the flights to take on a lunch break, or when you're looking for a quick getaway to some of the most scenic spots on earth. The following walkthroughs cover the most notable flights in this category. Each includes a suggested route, notes on some of the sights worth seeing, and a suggested landing field.

Along the Rockies

Area: Rocky Mountains, Montana, U.S.

Aircraft: Cessna 208B Caravan Amphibian

Landing: Glacier Park International Airport (KFCA)

Here you'll get the chance to take command of a Cessna 208B Caravan Amphibian and explore the scenery around Babb, Montana on the eastern slopes of the Rocky Mountains.

Radio Information

Glacier Park International Airport (KFCA)

STATION	FREQUENCY
Center	133.400
CTAF	123.000

NAV Radios

NAVAID	TYPE	FREQUENCY	DESIRED HEADING
FCA	VOR/DME	113.20	–
IFCA	ILS	111.50	017

The Flight

You begin this flight at 7,000 feet, just outside of Glacier National Park on the Montana–Alberta border. Although global warming has accounted for a dramatic reduction in the glacial coverage in the park, there are still many sensational views to be had, especially from the air. Park regulations require you to stay at least 2,000 feet AGL within its boundaries.

Highway 89 runs from your 5 o'clock to your 11 o'clock position and meets Glacier Route 3 just north of the large lake in front of you, splitting off to the southwest. Fly to the intersection and follow Glacier Route 3 along a heading of approximately 220. Ahead, you'll see the rugged Rocky Mountain peaks within the national park. Follow the road in and then freely explore the park. Although landing within the park is technically prohibited, Flathead Lake (approximately 15 miles south of Kalispell) offers unrestricted landing (and excellent fishing).

While in the park, use your GPS to guide you to N48° 55.32' W113° 50.85', where Mt. Cleveland towers above the park at almost 10,500 feet (see Figure 7.22). After you've explored the mountainside glaciers, jagged peaks, and innumerable river valleys, home in on the Kalispell (FCA) VOR and land at Glacier Park International Airport, which is uncontrolled.

Figure 7.22 *Mt. Cleveland offers an excellent view of the Waterton Lakes National Park, just over the U.S.–Canadian border.*

Giza at Dawn

Area: Pyramids of Giza, Cairo, Egypt

Aircraft: Cessna 172SP Skyhawk

Landing: Cairo International (HECA)

Greet the rising sun with the ancient Sphinx as you fly past the pyramids of Giza toward downtown Cairo in a Cessna 172SP. This flight will take you past some of the world's most impressive ancient structures. If you can't see as much as you want to see in the allotted time, don't be afraid to turn back the clock and get some more sunlight!

Radio Information

Cairo International Airport (HECA)

STATION	FREQUENCY
Approach	119.050
Tower	118.100
Ground	121.900

NAV Radios

NAVAID	TYPE	FREQUENCY	DESIRED HEADING
CVO	VOR/DME	115.20	–

The Flight

As with all scenic flights, this one begins in the air, with your aircraft facing directly toward the pyramid complex on the Giza Plateau. From southwest to northeast (away from you), you'll see the pyramids constructed by Pharaohs Menkaure, Khafre, and finally Khufu (also known as Cheops). To the southeast of Khufu's towering Great Pyramid—the largest Egyptian pyramid ever constructed and probably the most impressive man-made structure on Earth—lies the Sphinx (see Figure 7.23).

Figure 7.23 *The Great Sphinx has stood guard over the pyramids of the Giza Plateau for thousands of years.*

If you fly a heading of approximately 155 from the Great Pyramid, you will come across King Djoser's Step Pyramid at Saqqara, visible in the distance from the Giza Plateau. This pyramid is the oldest known large stone structure in the world. Imhotep, Djoser's vizier and architect, designed the building and oversaw its construction in 2630 BC.

After you've finished your tour of the pyramids, fly east to the Nile, and then direct to the Cairo (CVO) VOR. Request clearance and land at Cairo International Airport.

Hong Kong at Dusk

Area: Hong Kong, Hong Kong, China

Aircraft: Cessna 172SP Skyhawk

Landing: Hong Kong International (VHHH)

Tour Hong Kong in a Cessna 172SP as the sun sinks toward the horizon. This bustling metropolis is impressive at any time of day, but seeing the city lights while the rooftops are still lit by sunlight is truly impressive.

Radio Information

Hong Kong International Airport (VHHH)

STATION	FREQUENCY
Approach	119.100
Tower	118.400
Ground	121.600

NAV Radios

NAVAID	TYPE	FREQUENCY	DESIRED HEADING
SMT	VOR/DME	114.80	—

The Flight

You start this flight to the east of Hong Kong, with the city between you and the setting sun. The city lights will just be twinkling as the sun sets below the horizon, but you can still make out many features of the protected bay and the massive city surrounding it. The attraction here is the city itself, so feel free to dip down to rooftop level and explore the streets in this fantasy flight.

When you're done wandering the city, request landing clearance at Hong Kong International and set down. All runways at the airport are served by ILS, so don't worry about visibility slipping away as the sun sets. You can find all ILS frequencies listed by clicking the VHHH runway on your Map view, available in the World drop-down menu.

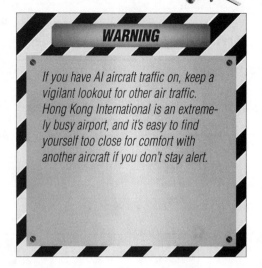

WARNING

If you have AI aircraft traffic on, keep a vigilant lookout for other air traffic. Hong Kong International is an extremely busy airport, and it's easy to find yourself too close for comfort with another aircraft if you don't stay alert.

Into the Canyon

Area: Grand Canyon, Arizona, U.S.

Aircraft: Extra 300S

Landing: McCarran International Airport (KLAS)

In this dream flight, you'll have the opportunity to take an Extra 300S for a spin over—and down into—the Grand Canyon. You can vary the level of challenge by choosing the altitude you'll limit yourself to; just remember that the lower you go, the better a flier you'll have to be!

Radio Information

McCarran International Airport (KLAS)

STATION	FREQUENCY
Approach	125.025
Tower	118.750
Ground	121.100

NAV Radios

NAVAID	TYPE	FREQUENCY	DESIRED HEADING
PGS	VOR/DME	112.00	–
LAS	VOR/DME	116.90	–

The Flight

It couldn't be a better day for flying—you've been blessed with clear weather, an aerobatic aircraft, and full permission to fly the Grand Canyon at any altitude and in any area that you want! You start the flight near the south rim. Make a left turn to head due north; this will bring you to a finger of the canyon just off Hopi Point, allowing you to drop smoothly down between the walls. At this point, you should choose an AGL altitude ceiling and stick to it— try 100-foot increments, starting at about 300 feet AGL. Nose over into the canyon along the valley and fly toward the Colorado River, at the heart of the Grand Canyon.

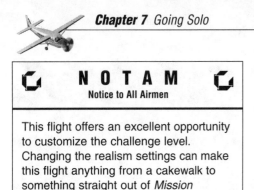

When you're directly over the river, drop into the central canyon by executing a right wingover. Pull up and right at the same time, bringing your nose up while simultaneously rolling the aircraft over onto its back. This will also bring the nose to the right. By the time you have turned through 90 degrees, you should be upside down and pointing east up the river (see Figure 7.24). At this point, execute the second half of a loop by pulling back on the stick and cutting your throttle to manage your airspeed. Use your ailerons and rudder to control the entry into the canyon, and level out at your target altitude. You should now be fast and low along the river, deep within Granite Gorge.

Figure 7.24 *Drop into the heart of the Grand Canyon with a wingover.*

Now it's time for smoke. Press the "I" key to get your smoke system started (there may be a slight delay before you start to see smoke behind you). Your path will take you through the heart of the Grand Canyon. You can either fly its entire length along the Colorado River or take one of the many secondary canyons. Try staying below your target altitude AGL at all times, breaking now and then to execute a loop or barrel roll as space permits. When you're ready to rest, tune in the Las Vegas (LAS) VOR, take a spin down the Las Vegas Strip, and land at McCarran International Airport.

McKinley Tour

Area: Mt. McKinley, Alaska, U.S.

Aircraft: Cessna 208B Caravan Amphibian

Landing: Talkeetna Airport (PATK)

Take a Cessna 208B Caravan Amphibian on a scenic tour of Alaska's Mount McKinley. Located about 100 miles northwest of Anchorage, Mt. McKinley sits in the center of Denali National Park. At 20,320 feet, it's the highest peak in North America.

Radio Information

Talkeetna Airport (PATK)

STATION	FREQUENCY
Center	125.550
CTAF	123.600

NAV Radios

NAVAID	TYPE	FREQUENCY	DESIRED HEADING
TKA	VOR/DME	116.20	–
BCQ	VOR	112.50	–
ANC	VOR/DME	114.30	–
EDF	DME	113.40	–

The Flight

You begin this flight headed straight for Mt. McKinley, which can be seen rising majestically out of the mist in the distance (see Figure 7.25). Continue on your initial heading (about 145 degrees) until you reach the peak. The mountaintop and surrounding valleys are covered in glaciers, so spend some time exploring the rugged landscape around the mountain as well. There are numerous rivers to follow throughout the area and several lakes upon which you can practice water landing and takeoff operations.

After you've explored the area, tune in the Talkeetna (TKA) VOR and head in for a landing. The airport does not have approach or tower services, so announce your intentions on the CTAF and land when it is safe to do so.

Figure 7.25 *Mt. McKinley is the highest peak in North America, making it hard to miss.*

Miami by Moonlight

Area: Miami, Florida, U.S.

Aircraft: Cessna 172SP Skyhawk

Landing: Miami International Airport (KMIA)

In this flight, you'll have the opportunity to cruise over Miami in a Cessna 172SP as the city sleeps. Explore the Bay of Biscayne, the Intercoastal Waterway, and the bright lights of downtown Miami by moonlight!

Radio Information

Miami International Airport (KMIA)

STATION	FREQUENCY
Approach	120.500
Tower	118.300
Ground	121.800

NAV Radios

NAVAID	TYPE	FREQUENCY	DESIRED HEADING
MI	NDB	248.0	–
DHP	VOR/DME	113.90	–

The Flight

Miami is known for its nightlife as well as its sunny beaches, and its virtual counterpart in *Flight Simulator 2002* does not disappoint. You begin the flight off the coast, in front of Miami Beach. The historic Art Deco district lies immediately to your front left, while the city of Miami proper shines brightly across the Bay of Biscayne. Further to your left is the MacArthur Causeway, and just south of it lies the bustling Port of Miami, the southernmost large island within the bay. You'll be able to identify it by the multiple rows of gigantic cargo cranes lining the slips along the island, as shown in Figure 7.26.

Figure 7.26 *Miami is one of the most active ports in America.*

Weave through the city to your heart's content, and then head in for a landing at Miami International Airport, just west of the city. You can't miss it, as the approach lights for runways 27L and 27R are clearly visible from downtown. On your way to the airport, fly over the historic Orange Bowl, home to the University of Miami Hurricanes. Touch down with clearance at KMIA to conclude a successful flight!

CHAPTER 8
Flying First Class

The following walkthroughs are detailed accounts of the commercial flight activities included in Flight Simulator 2002. Before tackling them, you should have already learned how to fly the "heavies" from the online documentation and the first chapters of this book. When you're ready to take on the role of a commercial captain, this chapter will serve as both a preflight briefing and as an in-flight kneeboard. It features all the flight plan, navigation, and radio frequency information needed to complete each activity.

European Airline Pilot

Area: Europe

Aircraft: 737-400

Flights: 6

Difficulty: Hard

The European Airline Pilot flight series puts you in the uniform of a flight captain working for the fictional Orbit Airlines. Your home airport is London Heathrow, from which you fly scheduled passenger routes throughout Europe. This week, you've got the Venice run, which will take you from England through France, and then on to Italy and Malta before returning to London. Flights span all times of day and visibility conditions, so expect your instrument skills to be tested.

Flight One: London to Paris

Origin: Heathrow International Airport (EGLL), Heathrow, England

Destination: Charles de Gaulle Airport (LFPG), Paris, France

Estimated Time En Route: 2 hours

Time of Day: Early morning

Weather: Clear/variable

Flight Plan: IFR

Route: EGLL OCK MID SFD WAFFU HARDY DPE33 DPE CRL28 VPM LFPG

Altitude: 37,000 feet

Landing: Charles de Gaulle ILS Runway 09

Your first flight with Orbit Airlines is the early morning trip from London to Paris. The weather is left at default clear conditions, although you may add to the realism by selecting real-world weather from the Weather menu after loading the activity.

Radio Information

London Heathrow International Airport (EGLL)

STATION	FREQUENCY
Ground	121.700
Tower	118.500

Charles de Gaulle Airport (LFPG)

STATION	FREQUENCY
Tower	119.250
Ground	118.100

NAV Radios

NAVAID	TYPE	FREQUENCY	DESIRED HEADING
OCK	VOR	115.30	181 (TO)
MID	VOR	114.00	208 (TO)
SFD	VOR	117.00	126 (TO)
DPE	VOR	115.80	145 (TO)
CGE	ILS	110.10	89

The Flight

You begin this flight holding short at London Heathrow Airport's runway 9, with your engines off. Get your aircraft started using the checklist provided in Chapter 2: Aircraft and Checklists, or hit Ctrl-E for auto-start. When ready, request clearance on your filed Instrument Flight Rules (IFR) flight plan. The runway extends off to the right of your nose, so head in this direction when cleared for takeoff. When ready for departure, use the standard takeoff procedures summarized in Chapter 2, or get the information on-screen by calling up your kneeboard (F10).

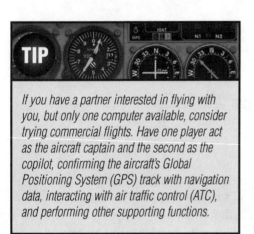

If you have a partner interested in flying with you, but only one computer available, consider trying commercial flights. Have one player act as the aircraft captain and the second as the copilot, confirming the aircraft's Global Positioning System (GPS) track with navigation data, interacting with air traffic control (ATC), and performing other supporting functions.

GPS will be used for your primary navigation along this and all commercial flights, but you should use standard navigation aids to confirm your position along each leg of the route. Bring up the GPS by clicking the satellite dish icon in the secondary instrumentation cluster (see Figure 8.1) or by pressing Shift-3. Note the orientation of the top of the GPS display—it can be adjusted using the Menu button on the GPS display to orient along your current heading, true north, or the desired track. Use whichever setting enables you to fly with the greatest precision. By default, your current heading is oriented upwards in the display.

Follow your flight plan as filed, using the GPS and the Flight Planner map to track your progress. Cruising altitudes vary throughout the trip, so check your designated altitude in the Navigation Log (NavLog) before each waypoint. The final waypoint takes you directly into Charles de Gaulle Airport, although you must fly a heading of approximately 115 to intercept

Figure 8.1 *The GPS button is located in the middle of the icon cluster on the lip of your instrument panel.*

the end of the Instrument Landing System (ILS) glide path. If you have trouble, tune to the RSO Non-Directional Radio Beacon (NDB) at 364.0 and home in on the end of the glide path for runway 9. Set your jet down gently and taxi to the gate to complete the flight.

Flight Two: Paris to Milan

Origin: Charles de Gaulle Airport (LFPG), Paris, France

Destination: Milan Malpensa Airport (LIMC), Milan, Italy

Estimated Time En Route: 3 hours

Time of Day: Morning

Weather: Clear/variable

Flight Plan: IFR

Route: LFPG EXIDU CLM BRY LUREN DIJ FRANE UIR30 PUNSA ARLES LIMC

Altitude: 41,000 feet

Landing: Milan Malpensa ILS Runway 35R

The next leg of your daily trip is from Paris to Milan. On this flight, you'll reach a cruising altitude of over 40,000 feet, well above the majestic Alps. The weather is set to the default clear conditions. If you want an added challenge, increase the realism by selecting real-world weather from the Weather menu after you load the activity.

Radio Information

Charles de Gaulle Airport (LFPG)

STATION	FREQUENCY
Tower	119.250
Ground	118.100

Milan Malpensa Airport (LIMC)

STATION	FREQUENCY
Tower	119.000
Ground	121.900

NAV Radios

NAVAID	TYPE	FREQUENCY	DESIRED HEADING
PGS	VOR	117.05	102 (FROM)
CLM	VOR	112.9	157 (TO)
BRY	NDB	277.0	160 (TO)
DIJ	VOR	113.50	135 (TO)
SRN	VOR	113.70	122 (TO)
MAL	VOR	111.20	141 (TO)
MLP	ILS	109.90	350

The Flight

As with the last flight, this activity begins with your aircraft already holding short, this time at runway 9 left at Charles de Gaulle Airport. Start your engines, go through the start-up checklist, and then get clearance for takeoff. You'll be navigating using GPS while tracking VHF Omnidirectional Range (VOR) information as a backup. When airborne, continue along the runway heading to the EXIDU intersection, where you'll be swinging right to head for Italy (see Figure 8.2).

As you approach the airport in Milan, follow ATC instructions to intercept the glide path for ILS runway 35. If you need assistance, the (MAL) NDB at the end of the runway approach corridor is at 364.0. Land and put into the gate with taxi clearance to complete a successful activity.

Figure 8.2 *Look out the left windows as you pass over the FRANE and VIR30 waypoints for a view of the Italian Alps.*

Flight Three: Milan to Venice

Origin: Milan Malpensa Airport (LIMC), Milan, Italy

Destination: Marco Polo Airport (LIPZ), Venice, Italy

Estimated Time En Route: 30 minutes

Time of Day: Early afternoon

Weather: Clear/variable

Flight Plan: IFR

Route: LIMC SRN ELTAR ADOSA VIC LIPZ

Altitude: 29,000 feet

Landing: Marco Polo ILS Runway 04R

The last flight on your first day of work for Orbit Airlines is the short hop from Milan to Venice's Marco Polo Airport. The flight is only a half-hour long—just enough time to reach 29,000 feet before starting a descent.

Radio Information

Milan Malpensa Airport (LIMC)

STATION	FREQUENCY
Ground	121.900
Tower	119.000

Marco Polo Airport (LIPZ)

STATION	FREQUENCY
Approach	120.400
Tower	121.200
Ground	121.700

NAV Radios

NAVAID	TYPE	FREQUENCY	DESIRED HEADING
SRN	VOR	113.70	87 (TO)
VIC	VOR	113.40	90 (TO)
VEN	NDB	379	LOM
VEN	ILS	110.30	42

The Flight

You begin this activity holding short of runway 17 left at Milan Malpensa Airport. By now, your start-up procedures should be second nature, but you should still use the checklists provided in Chapter 2: Aircraft and Checklists to reduce the chances of forgetting something. Get your required clearances from the tower and depart the airport (see Figure 8.3). After takeoff, clear the pattern and head for the Saronno (SRN) VOR, as shown on your GPS flight plan.

If you need help intercepting the glide path, the outer marker on the ILS runway is accompanied by an NDB at 379.0. Note that Venice has an approach frequency, unlike the other airports on your trip thus far. ATC should direct you into the glide path, where your ILS will guide you down for a safe landing. This puts you near the daily limit for flight time, so take the night off and enjoy the Venetian canals.

Figure 8.3 *Departing Milan Malpensa Airport, bound for the canals of Venice*

Flight Four: Venice to Palermo

Origin: Marco Polo Airport (LIPZ), Venice, Italy

Destination: Punta Raisi Airport (LICJ), Palermo, Italy

Estimated Time En Route: 4 hours, 30 minutes

Time of Day: Morning

Weather: Clear/variable

Flight Plan: IFR

Route: LIPZ AKADO BUSER ANC KUPAR PES KASTU TEA SOR DELER AMANO ROSAS LICJ

Altitude: 37,000 feet

Landing: Palermo ILS Runway 25L

After spending the night in Venice, you're assigned to fly from Marco Polo Airport (LIPZ) across the "boot" of Italy to Punta Raisi Airport (LICJ) in Palermo, the largest city on the island of Sicily. This is the first of three legs today that will eventually return you to England.

Radio Information

Marco Polo Airport (LIPZ)

STATION	FREQUENCY
Ground	121.700
Tower	121.200

Punta Raisi Airport (LICJ)

STATION	FREQUENCY
Approach	118.650
Tower	119.050

NAV Radios

NAVAID	TYPE	FREQUENCY	DESIRED HEADING
ANC	VOR	110.65	193 (TO)
PES	VOR	115.90	154 (TO)
TEA	VOR	112.90	187 (TO)
SOR	VOR	112.20	158 (TO)
PAL	VOR	112.30	199 (TO)
RAI	ILS	109.50	247

The Flight

You begin this flight holding short of runway 4 right at Marco Polo Airport in Venice. Start up, get your clearances, and take off. In the absence of a standard departure procedure, fly the airport traffic pattern to reach your desired heading of 148, headed for the AKADO intersection. Use your GPS to fly to the intersection, which has no navaids related to your approach course.

Ascend to your cruising altitude at flight level 370 and follow your GPS course as filed. You'll have short breaks between waypoints on this trip, which makes several course changes due to the busy airspace over the Italian peninsula. Begin your descent after the DELER intersection and intercept the glide slope for runway 24 with a final course of about 180 degrees, or as directed by ATC. Once on the ground, contact ground control and taxi to the gate as cleared.

N O T A M
Notice to All Airmen

This is the first flight that requires complete reliance upon your GPS equipment to fly the flight plan as filed. If you've been relying too heavily on standard radio beacon navigation, now is the time to remove your training wheels!

Flight Five: Palermo to Malta

Origin: Punta Raisi Airport (LICJ), Palermo, Italy

Destination: Malta International Airport (LMML), Malta, Italy

Estimated Time En Route: 30 minutes

Time of Day: Afternoon

Weather: Clear/variable

Flight Plan: IFR

Route: LICJ PAL MARON EKOLA GZO LMML

Altitude: 29,000 feet

Landing: Malta ILS Runway 32

This short flight takes you from Punta Raisi Airport (LICJ) in Palermo to Malta International Airport (LMML), on the island of Malta.

Radio Information

Punta Raisi Airport (LICJ)

STATION	FREQUENCY
Tower	119.050

Malta International Airport (LMML)

STATION	FREQUENCY
Approach	121.000
Tower	118.900

NAV Radios

NAVAID	TYPE	FREQUENCY	DESIRED HEADING
PAL	VOR	112.30	157 (FROM)
GZO	VOR	115.70	157 (TO)
MLT	NDB	395.0	128 (TO)
LM	ILS	110.50	314

The Flight

You'll leave Punta Raisi Airport with another apron start-up. Circle around the airport and head for your first waypoint at the Palermo VOR (PAL), being careful to stay in the traffic pattern as you round the airport. When you reach PAL, settle on the GPS track and continue to ascend. You may never quite reach your cruising altitude before starting to descend, at the EKOLA waypoint (see Figure 8.4).

Figure 8.4 *This short flight precludes attaining a cruising altitude of flight level 290.*

Your approach is just about the reciprocal heading of your landing runway, so enter the traffic pattern at Malta International and circle at five miles to intercept the glide path. Naturally, follow ATC instructions and enter the landing queue, if there is one. Beware of surprise or sudden runway clearance changes! Malta is a nice airport to have your dynamic scenery turned on, as you can view moderate levels of air traffic. When it's your turn to land, put the plane down and taxi to the gate to complete the activity.

Flight Six: Malta to London

Origin: Malta International Airport (LMML), Malta, Italy

Destination: Heathrow International Airport (EGLL), Heathrow, England

Estimated Time En Route: 2 hours, 45 minutes

Time of Day: Evening

Weather: Clear/variable

Flight Plan: IFR

Route: LMML MLT GZO PANTA TALNA KIMKO TRP KAPIL QUENN MADKA AJO MERLU DIVUL NIZ TEKOT TDP PITOR ATN AVLON OKRIX TELBO MEL BERAP EDULI OL VPM CRL28 DPE DPE33 HARDY WAFFU SFD MID EGLL

Altitude: 39,000 feet

Landing: London Heathrow ILS Runway 27L

The flight from Malta to London is the last leg of your roundtrip route, bringing you back to Heathrow. This night flight shouldn't be very different from the daytime flights, as by now you should be able to rely completely on instruments for navigation and landing. For an added challenge, use real-world weather or create a storm using the advanced Weather menu.

Radio Information

Malta International Airport (LMML)

STATION	FREQUENCY
Tower	118.900

London Heathrow International Airport (EGLL)

STATION	FREQUENCY
Approach	119.725
Tower	118.500
Ground	121.700

NAV Radios

NAVAID	TYPE	FREQUENCY	DESIRED HEADING
MLT	NDB	395.0	134 (TO)
GZO	NDB	320.0	310 (TO)
ATN	VOR	114.90	330 (TO)
MEL	VOR	109.80	315 (TO)
OL	VOR	111.20	336 (TO)
DPE	VOR	115.80	329 (TO)
SFD	VOR	117.00	325 (TO)
MID	VOR	114.00	306 (TO)
ILL	ILS	109.50	274

The Flight

Malta International will be left behind via runway 6 at dusk. You start holding short of the runway and shut down, as usual. Run through your checks and initiate a standard start. Avoid the temptation to rush through things in order to get back home as soon as possible—this is sometimes called "barn fever" or "get home-itis" and can lead to errors or omissions. Get in the air, and start in on your lengthy flight plan using your GPS.

As this is a night flight, there won't be much to see on the way. With only minor course changes along your route, you can use your autopilot most of the way, changing the desired heading settings at each waypoint to bring the airplane onto its new course. Remember to complete each controller handoff along the way to retain IFR flight services. Begin your descent at the DPE33 waypoint and intercept the glide path after you round the MID VOR. Pay attention to the altimeter settings relayed from ATC, and set your altimeter accordingly so that you can land without visual reference. London Heathrow Airport is at 80 feet above sea level. Touch down gently (as in Figure 8.5), taxi to the gate, and go home for some well-deserved rest!

Figure 8.5 *A comfortable evening landing is one of the joys of being a commercial captain.*

Cargo Pilot

Area: Pacific Rim to North America

Aircraft: 747-400

Flights: 4

Difficulty: Hard

As a Boeing 747-400 captain for Global Freightways, you provide on-demand hauling for business and airline clients around the world. Unlike standard express mail services with regularly scheduled routes, Global Freightways flights are chartered for specific high-priority shipments. Whether it's a rush delivery of aircraft parts to a grounded jet, containers full of TVs, or relief supplies bound for a hurricane-ravaged nation, you get the job done—fast.

Flight One: Tokyo to Hong Kong

Origin: New Tokyo International Airport (RJAA), Narita, Japan

Destination: Hong Kong International Airport (VHHH), Hong Kong, China

Estimated Time En Route: 3 hours, 45 minutes

Time of Day: Early morning

Weather: Clear/variable

Flight Plan: IFR

Route: RJAA KOZ FLUTE HANWA KRE USUKI RINDO ESBIS BOLOD SALMI QUEEN SEEDY INDIA IKATA HETIA VHHH

Altitude: 43,000

Landing: As directed

Your first flight as a commercial cargo captain is an early morning priority delivery from New Tokyo International Airport (RJAA) to Hong Kong International (VHHH). You'll be up before the sun on this flight, so bring along some coffee.

Radio Information

New Tokyo International Airport (RJAA)

STATION	FREQUENCY
ATIS	128.250
Delivery	121.900

STATION	FREQUENCY
Ground	121.800
Tower	118.200
Departure	124.200

Hong Kong International Airport (VHHH)

STATION	FREQUENCY
Approach	119.100
Tower	118.400
Ground	121.600

NAV Radios

NAVAID	TYPE	FREQUENCY	DESIRED HEADING
NRE	VOR	117.30	249 (FROM)
KRE	VOR	113.70	252 (TO) 254 (FROM)
LC	NDB	390.0	241 (TO)
ISR	ILS (7R)	109.30	73
IFL	ILS (25L)	108.90	253
IZSL	ILS (7L)	111.10	73
ITFR	ILS (25R)	110.90	253

The Flight

All flights in the Cargo Pilot series begin as shown in Figure 8.6, at the cargo terminal of the departure airport with the aircraft shut down and ready for engine start. Use the start-up procedures found in the checklist provided in Chapter 2: Aircraft and Checklists to walk through each step of a preflight inspection and start-up, taxi, and takeoff procedures.

After start-up, contact clearance delivery and get pushback clearance. Walk through the taxi checklist as you head for the departure runway, clearing each step with ATC as you go. It's hard to get lost, as the automated ATC communications menu gives you all of the proper options at the right times. Consult the v-speeds for the 747, detailed in Chapter 2, or by calling up your kneeboard using the F10 key. When you're familiar with your aircraft and cleared for departure, throttle up and take off into the early morning sky.

You will use the GPS as your primary means of navigation on this flight, as much of it is over water and does not make use of ground-based navaids. Orient the top of the GPS dis-

Figure 8.6 *The Tokyo skyline is visible on the horizon in the early dawn light.*

play in whatever direction is most natural to you by using the GPS Menu button, and follow your intended track according to your flight plan. ATC will hand you off to new controllers at the appropriate times. Eventually, you'll be cleared for landing in Hong Kong. Tune to the ILS frequency (listed above) that corresponds to the runway you're cleared for, and follow the glide slope in for a landing to complete the first commercial cargo flight.

Flight Two: Hong Kong to San Francisco

Origin: Hong Kong International Airport (VHHH), Hong Kong, China

Destination: San Francisco International Airport (KSFO), San Francisco, CA

Estimated Time En Route: 14 hours, 30 minutes.

Time of Day: Early afternoon to morning

Weather: Clear/variable

Flight Plan: IFR

Route: Extensive (see Flight Planner for more)

Altitude: 41,000 feet

Landing: San Francisco ILS Runway 28R

This is the longest of all the flights included with *Flight Simulator 2002*. The flight from Hong Kong to San Francisco wraps around the entire northern half of the Pacific Rim, crossing over China, Russia, the Bering Strait, Alaska, western Canada, and the northwestern United States. The trip takes well over 14 hours, and if you are flying with realistic weather, it can take even longer. This type of flight would be flown with rotating aircrews in real life, so don't hesitate in the least to save the flight partway through, as realism will not be sacrificed.

Radio Information

Hong Kong International Airport (VHHH)

STATION	FREQUENCY
ATIS	128.200
Delivery	129.900
Ground	121.600
Tower	118.400

San Francisco International Airport (KSFO)

STATION	FREQUENCY
Approach	120.350
Tower	120.500
Ground	121.800

NAV Radios

NAVAID	TYPE	FREQUENCY	DESIRED HEADING
POU	VOR	114.10	319 (TO)
WA	NDB	342.0	36 (TO)
NS	NDB	333.0	13 (TO)
LIG	VOR	112.40	348 (TO)
LKO	VOR	115.80	6 (TO)
ZF	NDB	369.0	27 (TO)
ZHO	VOR	115.50	7 (TO)
WXI	VOR	115.70	9 (TO)
SJW	VOR	117.70	359 (TO)
KR	NDB	314.0	357 (TO)
CD	NDB	422.0	52 (TO)

NAVAID	TYPE	FREQUENCY	DESIRED HEADING
LR	NDB	215.0	62 (TO)
DW	NDB	768.0	57 (TO)
LS	NDB	662.0	66 (TO)
RQ	NDB	458.0	74 (TO)
IJ	NDB	394.0	78 (TO)
QI	NDB	335.0	55 (TO)
XR	NDB	615.0	45 (TO)
TA	NDB	995.0	61 (TO)
FDV	NDB	529.0	72 (TO)
JNR	NDB	382.0	87 (TO)
VTR	NDB	35.0	90 (TO)
CMQ	NDB	338.0	99 (TO)
HBK	NDB	362.0	78 (TO)
BKA	VOR	113.8	96 (TO)
ANH	VOR	117.10	100 (TO)
YZT	VOR	112.00	126 (TO)
TOU	VOR	112.20	119 (TO)
HQM	VOR	117.70	153 (TO)
OED	VOR	113.60	148 (TO)
RBL	VOR	115.70	150 (TO)
IGWQ	ILS	111.70	282 (TO)

The Flight

This flight commences at the cargo terminal in Hong Kong, awaiting start-up. Use the start-up checklist provided in Chapter 2: Aircraft and Checklists to get you to the runway, requesting your clearances from ATC as necessary. Hong Kong has a very busy schedule, so you'll see plenty of activity if you have dynamic scenery and air traffic turned on!

TIP

One way to step up the challenge level on this flight is to introduce real-world weather, which will vary by region and can be quite bad over the poorly named Pacific Ocean, which is anything but pacific!

You can use your GPS for navigating throughout this flight, although the route was plotted using high-altitude airways. The specified route does, in fact, represent an approximation of a great circle route, but if you'd like to take the more direct path, simply replot to use GPS direct routing. This will draw a single great circle line to San Francisco from Hong Kong, allowing you to cut down your transit time considerably. The only drawback is that you'll be over water for most of the flight (as shown in Figure 8.7), which makes for tougher navigation if your GPS goes out and a short option list should you face a forced landing.

Figure 8.7 *A 747 leaves the Asian coast behind.*

Follow whichever flight plan you plan to use with your GPS. Employ navaid stations to verify your position at each waypoint. You'll be handed off to alternate ATC centers along the way, so make sure that you keep up with your COM radio tuning. You can use the ATC communication feature to automatically tune your radios, if you respond at the proper time. On approach to San Francisco, make sure you get an altimeter update so that you can reliably fly an instrument landing. The Bay Area is often fogged in, making it very important to have a localized altitude reading.

Flight Three: San Francisco to Dallas–Fort Worth

Origin: San Francisco International Airport (KSFO), San Francisco, CA

Destination: Dallas–Fort Worth International Airport (KDFW), Dallas, Texas

Estimated Time En Route: 3 hours, 30 minutes.

Time of Day: Early afternoon

Weather: Clear/variable

Flight Plan: IFR

Route: KSFO OAK ECA OAL ILC MLF FMN LVS ABI ACT KDFW (navaids only)

Altitude: 41,000 feet

Landing: Dallas ILS Runway 17R

With the benefit of a much-needed rest in San Francisco after last night's Pacific crossing, you are called upon to deliver a high-priority load to Dallas–Fort Worth International. The plane is loaded up by the early afternoon, so without further ado, you're off to Texas.

Radio Information

San Francisco International Airport (KSFO)

STATION	FREQUENCY
Delivery	118.200
Ground	121.800
Tower	120.500
Departure	120.900

Dallas–Fort Worth International Airport (KDFW)

STATION	FREQUENCY
Approach	118.100
Tower	124.150
Ground	121.650

NAV Radios

NAVAID	TYPE	FREQUENCY	DESIRED HEADING
OAK	VOR	116.80	32 (TO)
ECA	VOR	116.00	66 (TO)
OAL	VOR	117.70	71 (TO)
ILC	VOR	116.30	68 (TO)
MLF	VOR	112.10	69 (TO)
FMN	VOR	115.30	96 (TO)

NAVAID	TYPE	FREQUENCY	DESIRED HEADING
LVS	VOR	117.30	103 (TO)
ABI	VOR	113.70	143 (TO)
ACT	VOR	115.30	95 (TO)
IJHZ	ILS	111.35	174

The Flight

This flight commences at the cargo terminal of San Francisco International Airport. Be careful with your clearances if you have dynamic scenery turned on, as this is one extremely busy facility, and you can find yourself in the path of a jumbo jet if you wander out of place. Taxiing can be made easier by pressing Shift-] to get a top-down view of your progress (as shown in Figure 8.8). ATC can also help by providing progressive taxi instructions.

Figure 8.8 *This overhead view comes in handy when taxiing at an unfamiliar airport.*

You can use navigation radios for the entirety of your flight, with the GPS used as a backup. Follow your progress along the navigation aid chart provided above, but use the GPS to track your flight plan. On approach to Dallas–Fort Worth, you can use the FL NDB at 219.0 to intercept the ILS glide path for a landing on runway 17R. Try to establish a heading to intercept the localizer that shows the FL NDB 30 degrees off the inbound localizer course. You'll be landing in the late afternoon, but with the long summer hours, there will still be plenty of light left in the sky. Switch to the ground control frequency and get taxi clearance to the cargo terminal to conclude another successful flight.

Flight Four: Dallas–Fort Worth to Atlanta

Origin: Dallas–Fort Worth International Airport (KDFW), Dallas, Texas

Destination: Atlanta International Airport (KATL), Atlanta, Georgia

Estimated Time En Route: 1 hour, 45 minutes

Time of Day: Early afternoon

Weather: Clear/variable

Flight Plan: IFR

Route: KDFW CVE TORNN CRIED LFK TBEND AEX MCB MEI JAMMR WEONE KATL

Altitude: 41,000 feet

Landing: Atlanta ILS Runway 9R

Your next flight as a cargo captain is a short regional flight to Atlanta, a commercial hub in the southern United States. This flight is relatively straightforward, but can be complicated by high temperatures or even gale-force winds in tornado season. If you're up to the challenge, use real-world weather for the flight or try altering the time or season.

Radio Information

Dallas–Fort Worth International Airport (KDFW)

STATION	FREQUENCY
ATIS	123.775
Delivery	128.250
Ground	121.650
Tower	124.150
Departure	118.100

Atlanta (KATL)

STATION	FREQUENCY
Approach	118.350
Tower	119.100
Ground	121.750

NAV Radios

NAVAID	TYPE	FREQUENCY	DESIRED HEADING
CVE	VOR	116.20	86 (TO) 159 (FROM)
LFK	VOR	112.10	97 (TO) 81 (FROM)
AEX	VOR	116.10	82 (TO)
MCB	VOR	116.70	83 (TO)
MEI	VOR	117.00	46 (TO) 59 (FROM)
ATL	VOR	116.90	80 (TO)
IFUN	ILS	108.90	92

The Flight

Dallas–Fort Worth International Airport is a large, sprawling hub (see Figure 8.9), so you may need progressive taxi instructions if you don't have a terminal chart handy (you can find one for free at http://www.airnav.com/airport/DFW). Depart the airport with IFR clearance and exit the busy traffic pattern before heading for your first waypoint. You can use GPS or navaids to fly your flight plan on this activity, as the course is well marked by VOR stations along the way.

Figure 8.9 *Dallas–Fort Worth International serves over 2,500 aircraft a day.*

Your approach course into Atlanta closely matches the runway heading, and you will likely be cleared for a direct approach. If you get off your intended track, use the ATL VOR at 116.90 to find your way back to the airport. Approach with a heading of 90 to intercept the glide path. When you're centered on the path, follow it down for a smooth landing. Ease up to the gate to complete another successful delivery.

CHAPTER 9
Sharing the Sky

Microsoft Flight Simulator 2002 *comes ready for multiplayer flying on MSN Gaming Zone (www.zone.com), over the Internet, or on a local area network (LAN). These venues allow you to fly in formation with other aircraft, participate in an airport fly-in, or conduct any of the other multiplayer ideas outlined in this chapter. Some previously unpublished information on the VATSIM online ATC network—which offers round-the-clock, live air traffic control across the globe—has also been included. All of this is available without any additional program purchases, so complete your crosschecks and read on to take your flying to the ultimate level.*

Setting up a Multiplayer Flight

First, we'll help you set up a standard multiplayer session. If you've never played a multi-player game before, now is the perfect time to start. Unlike combat-oriented games, which are by nature confrontational, the people you meet in flight simulator sessions are fellow virtual pilots looking for an enjoyable time in shared sim-airspace. If you have friends with *Flight Simulator 2002*, you can fly with them, even if you aren't connected to a LAN. Below, we'll help you through your first multiplayer experience.

The MSN Gaming Zone

The MSN Gaming Zone is the easiest way for a pilot to find a friend in the air. Simply surf over to www.zone.com or use the link provided in the simulator via the multiplayer screen (as shown in Figure 9.1). During your first visit to the Zone, you'll be given the chance to automatically download the matchmaking software. It will automatically install after the download, and when you're ready (you'll be asked if you can see a playing card symbol), you can go back to the *Flight Simulator 2002* lobby to join or start a game.

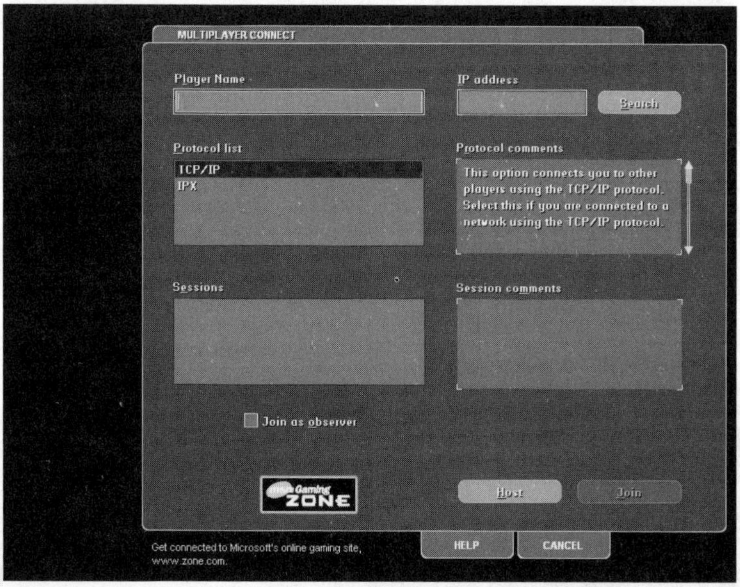

Figure 9.1 *Flight sessions on the Zone are easy to set up.*

Once in the Zone lobby, you'll see three main areas on your screen. The main section, anchored on the left side, is the game table display, which shows all those players currently in the air. The right-hand window features a list of every player in the lobby at the time, divided into groups according to what each is doing (looking for a game, waiting at one of the tables for a game to start, or actually flying). At the top, you may see people with a * or + before their names, or maybe an "@zone" at the end of their names. These are the people who help run the Zone, and they will assist you if you have any questions or problems. The last window is the real-time chat interface that runs across the bottom of the screen. Most of the players conversing here will be looking for a flight, so you'll see game hosts advertising their settings.

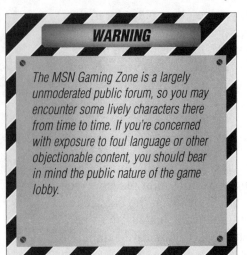

WARNING

The MSN Gaming Zone is a largely unmoderated public forum, so you may encounter some lively characters there from time to time. If you're concerned with exposure to foul language or other objectionable content, you should bear in mind the public nature of the game lobby.

Latency is the most important thing to consider in a Zone game. Each player's name is accompanied by a little colored latency meter, which ranges from several bright green bars (the best) to several bright red bars (the worst). Latency is the time it takes for a signal to travel over the Internet between two computers, and the higher it is, the worse it is for multiplayer flights. You'll notice that each game table also has a set of these bars next to it (see Figure 9.2). This represents your latency to the game host, which is critical. If you have a slow connection to the host, everything in the game will run slowly for you. Therefore, it is best to select a host showing a bright green connection.

When you find an acceptable game, click the table to join it (some tables are grayed out, which means that their flights are already in session and cannot be joined). When your host starts your multiplayer session, *Flight Simulator 2002* will automatically launch and you'll

Figure 9.2 *The MSN Gaming Zone windows*

find yourself in the cockpit. While you may adjust your aircraft and other options once you are in the simulation, you should take note of any special restrictions or instructions stated by the host, and do your best to comply with the game type established. If you're interested in doing something different from what the host has in mind, it's better to find a game more suitable to your tastes.

Some Zone sessions will also offer ongoing connections to flights in progress. You can join these at any time, as long as there is room. These flights are usually fly-ins to a given airport. You may even find the host acting as an air traffic controller at the airport, and you'll be asked to interact with that player as if he or she were the tower! This can lead to some very satisfying flights, as a live controller helps you get the full experience of a real flight. For more than just a brief taste of these operations, turn to the end of this chapter for a tour of the VATSIM network.

> **WARNING**
>
> Retune the Flight Simulator settings for multiplayer flights! The game takes a severe performance hit in multiplayer mode, so settings that are perfect for solo flights slow down multiplayer action. Record your solo settings, and then bump everything down one level to increase performance when sharing the sky online.

Direct Connections

If you're on a LAN or are looking to hook up with a few specific pilots, you can use direct connections to bypass the Zone matchmaking service. In order to do this, you'll have to know your IP (Internet Protocol) address. To determine what your IP address is, go to the Start menu from your Windows desktop and click Run. Then type `winipcfg` to bring up the IP Configuration display, shown in Figure 9.3. If you're using a cable modem or other persistent connection to the Internet, you may have more than one adapter, so click the drop-down box and select the one that has the words "PCI" or "Ethernet" in it.

Once you've selected the proper adapter, take a look at the window that says "IP Address" and jot it down. This is the address your friends will need to connect to your computer. Please note that if you are behind a firewall (like the computer in Figure 9.3), you'll have to contact your network administrator to help you determine your IP address. Your Internet service provider should also be able to provide your true IP address.

Now that you have your IP address, it's time to start the simulation. Go to the multiplayer screen, select TCP/IP, and click OK. This takes you to the host screen, where you can name your flight session, enter a short description of the upcoming flight, and control the maximum number of pilots in the simulation. You can even choose to be an observer, either a silent watcher or an air traffic controller.

When you've configured the session to your liking, click OK again to start the session. After a short wait, your game will be active and you can get started. Let your friends know that the session is online, and give them the IP address so that they will be able to "find"

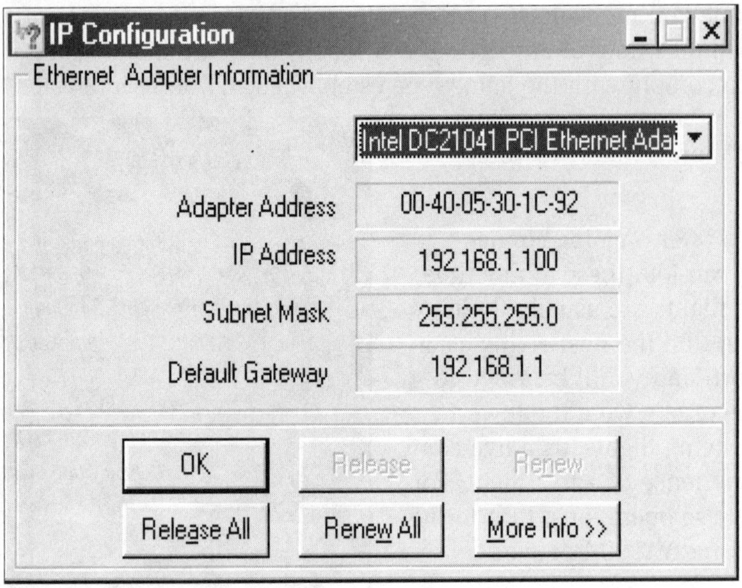

Figure 9.3 Here's how to display your IP address in one easy step.

your computer online. You'll soon see them in the game, and a chat box will open up allowing you to send and receive messages. Start at the same airport and you'll be able to see each other in the game!

Multiplayer Activities

After you're connected with one or more human pilots, the sky's the limit in terms of gaming options! Even without any additional utilities or add-on programs, you can enjoy a wide range of activities that are only available in multiplayer flights. You can race fellow pilots in a flat-out speed challenge, or chase each other through narrow canyons or down city streets in a white-knuckle obstacle course run. This is the kind of thing that *Flight Simulator* is better suited for than even real flying—as you'd never want to risk life and limb flying through downtown San Francisco in real life!

Course Racing

Any speed challenge over a designated course can make a good multiplayer activity. Traditionally, air races are conducted over an oval course with four pylons. You can step up the challenge level by varying the turns, thus creating an obstacle course. Whatever you decide, make it simple enough for racers to concentrate on flying their planes, not remembering if they're supposed to take a left or a right at the Statue of Liberty.

To set up a course race, specify an easily identified set of course boundaries using landmarks. You can even build your own racing course with the Professional Edition's gMax tools by placing course markers as scenery objects along the path of your choice. A racetrack is formed by the outer edges of your boundary landmarks. For example, you can create a Manhattan course that starts at the Statue of Liberty, goes under the Brooklyn Bridge, and then comes back around the Empire State Building (see Figure 9.4). These three simple landmarks are easy to remember, but make for a challenging course. For even more of an adventure, you can specify that it all has to be done while flying below 400 feet! Thanks to that additional rule, your pilots will have to figure out how to get through downtown traffic just to reach all of their landmarks.

Figure 9.4 *This King Air goes where no Beechcraft has gone before!*

To start a course race, have all pilots complete a pace lap around the course in close formation at approximately 75% throttle. When you pass the start line, throttle up and go three laps! You can vary the laps as desired, but note that a winner will usually be apparent after as few as two trips around the course. The winning pilot will always be the one who knows how to maintain speed through the corners. Most pilots don't realize how much speed they waste when they bank their aircraft. Use precisely coordinated turns and careful altitude management to get the most out of your engine. With practice, you'll be the first to the checkered flag.

Drag Racing

The drag race has a simple concept: be the first plane to reach a specified destination from a common starting point. The usual way to start this challenge is to position all planes at a large airport with two parallel runways. All pilots start at the base of one of the runways, and at the "go" signal, they may release their parking brakes. Once the race is on, each pilot attempts to be the first one to land at a specified destination. Whoever lands first is declared the winner!

NOTAM
Notice to All Airmen

A certain element of trust and honesty is required when participating in a drag race. Since a host cannot prohibit slew mode or an increased simulation rate, an unscrupulous pilot could use these tools to cheat. Feel free to use the replay feature to look for pilots who suddenly went from 150 knots to 300 knots.

To succeed at drag racing, you must have a strong understanding of your plane's performance. A drag race takes the most skill if it is more than 20 miles in length, as this will allow pilots who optimize their climb rates and cruise altitudes to pass those who are just mashing the throttle and going for broke. Make smooth maneuvers to avoid bleeding speed, establish your optimum climb speed, and head for your best cruising altitude. Close to the ground, planes have to push through thicker air, and parasitic drag is a greater problem. Up too high, the air is thinner and your available horsepower decreases. Knowing the sweet spot between the two is the key to drag-race victory.

Formation Flying

Trying to maintain formation while flying from one point to another is harder than it sounds, especially if you throw in some required maneuvers. Even the gentlest bank then becomes a serious challenge, as the turn speeds and bank angles will not be the same for each plane in the formation. You'll gain a new appreciation for military pilots when you try formation flying yourself.

NOTAM
Notice to All Airmen

If you're up to a real challenge, try putting on an airshow with a few standard aerobatic maneuvers. These might include loops, barrel rolls, or high-speed passes. A few rounds of formation flying will show you why there are only a few skilled exhibition teams in the world that perform formation flying.

The basic building block of formation flying is the element, a two-ship formation consisting of a flight leader and a wingman (see Figure 9.5). The standard element configuration is to have the wingman behind and to the left of the leader, or approximately 210 degrees off the leader's nose. Spacing depends on the situation; try 100 feet for a good taste of the challenge of formation flight.

To maintain formation, the leader should fly as smoothly as possible. Autopilot is an excellent way to maintain a steady heading and altitude. Communicate all maneuvers before they are executed, and then give a "go" signal to begin the maneuver. The wingman should focus

Figure 9.5 *Two Extras line up for takeoff just before a formation flight.*

on a single point on the leader's aircraft, like a wingtip or the point at which the leading edge of the vertical stabilizer meets the fuselage, and try to keep that spatially affixed to a reference point on his or her own cockpit or HUD. Additional wingmen in the formation should do the same, but fixing on the plane in front of them instead of on the leader.

Guts and Glory

For some serious barnstorming, try a follow-the-leader flight in an area with dense scenery. A city like New York, Chicago, or San Francisco makes a perfect choice. Select a maneuverable aircraft (all pilots should fly the same plane) and designate one of you as the leader. Line up in single file with a spacing of about 500–1,000 feet between each aircraft; modify this as necessary, depending on the degree of difficulty you want in your flights. If additional pilots are in the session, they should line up behind each other as well, because if everyone follows on the leader's wing, it won't take long before two planes try to share the same piece of the sky when shooting through a tight spot.

Using all the tricks in his or her hat, the leader should try to execute hard-to-follow maneuvers through tight passages, under low bridges, around sharp turns, and all manner of other challenging terrain (see Figure 9.6). Don't execute more than one or two maneuvers in rapid succession, or your trailing pilots will lose track of you. The idea is to challenge the followers to actually keep pace with you, not to lose them. It's much more fun to "lose" your chase planes against the side of the Empire State Building than it is to have them break off pursuit on Madison Avenue because they couldn't figure out where you went!

Figure 9.6 *Lead your chase planes through tight spots.*

Give each pilot about five to 10 minutes at the head of the pack, and then rotate to another flyer. If a leader crashes, it's time for the next person in line to step up to the cockpit. You can also run more cutthroat flights by using attrition rules—meaning that if you crash, you go to the end of the line. In this way you'll certainly rotate the rear ranks, but it may be frustrating for some pilots who might not get a turn at the front.

The VATSIM Network

The *Flight Simulator* series has an immense following worldwide, including some fans who happen to be capable programmers, network engineers, and other computer-savvy types. This combination has led to some incredible fan-created add-ons and third-party utilities over the years. Perhaps the most impressive of them all, however, are the virtual air traffic control (ATC) networks that have been created.

The concept sounds incredible at first—real people around the world are at this very moment standing by, providing real-time global ATC services for virtual pilots flying various versions of *Microsoft Flight Simulator* (see Figure 9.7). All of the pilots are in the same world, and they can see and interact with each other. All of the ATC personnel are volunteers, all of the software needed to hook up to the network is free, and all of the pilots are filing and flying their own flight plans.

A group called VATSIM (short for Virtual Air Traffic/Simulated) is the leading virtual ATC network at the time of this writing. The network is relatively new, having just launched this

Figure 9.7 *This Mooney Bravo has just been cleared for takeoff by the tower.*

year. VATSIM is staffed entirely by volunteers who use donated servers and Internet access. It also offers relatively easy log-ons, optional real-time voice communication, and 24-hour (virtual) worldwide activity. You can find it at `www.vatsim.net`. The service requires pilot registration, but it is free, instantaneous, and open to all virtual pilots.

Essential Tools

A few additional programs are required to get on the VATSIM network, which are all free and readily available on the Internet. The following list will get you started. Note that there are also direct links to these and several other programs on the VATSIM site.

SquawkBox

`www.simclients.com`

SquawkBox is a management program that helps you interact with the other pilots on the VATSIM network. It handles your communications, your flight plan, and most of your interaction with air traffic control. It even tunes your radios for you! It's a little hard to manage, however, because it doesn't behave like a standard window (you can't click and drag the window). The way to get around this is to click and drag its corners to resize it. Just expand one corner to where you want it to end up, and then take the opposite corner and drag it down until the window is in an appropriate spot.

FSNavigator

www.fsnavigator.com

This program is an extremely useful tool that allows you to create detailed flight plans using a fully graphical interface (shown in Figure 9.8). You can then export these flight plans to SquawkBox, which is used for submission to VATSIM's controllers. FSNavigator also makes an excellent companion to any *Flight Simulator* flight, even in the solo mode, as it features handy navigation tools over and above the ones that ship with the game.

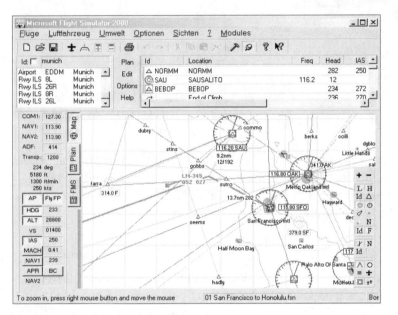

Figure 9.8 *Get detailed airport information from FSNavigator.*

Roger Wilco

www.rogerwilco.com

Roger Wilco has become a staple of the Internet gaming world. It offers real-time voice communication with any number of people, anywhere in the world. This free software requires a microphone, and it is best used with a headset mic for optimal performance. Don't overpower your microphone—the most common problem on voice communications is a mic that is too close to the speaker's mouth, resulting in garbled transmissions. Microphones are available for a reasonable price—as little as $8.

Hooking Up

Once you have obtained the tools you need, you're ready for your first controlled flight! Figure 9.9 shows the VATSIM network page that lists all controllers and pilots currently online. Find an airport (by its airport code) with one or more controllers working it, so that you'll have someone to interact with. To begin your session, start *Flight Simulator 2002*, begin a flight, call up FSNavigator with the F9 key, and then create a flight plan to, from, or around the chosen airport. If your flight originates or terminates at a heavily staffed airport, you'll get different controllers for delivery, ground, tower, approach, and even center control!

Figure 9.9 Shopping for an airport on the VATSIM network directory

After your flight plan has been created, export it to SquawkBox using the menus in the center of the flight plan text windows (near the top of the FSNavigator display). Now, use *Flight Simulator 2002* to slew over to a gate and save your flight (use "temp" or some other recyclable name—unless you intend to take off from this airport often). By getting off the runway, you won't suddenly pop into the game world in front of, say, a 747 on short final. Once you're in position, start a multiplayer *Flight Simulator 2002* session as the host. Naming conventions for the session are described on the VATSIM Web site.

Start SquawkBox and go through the start-up sequence, entering your name, connecting to the network,

TIP

Note that some controllers have a "_V_" in their names, which designates their use of the Roger Wilco voice software (see above). Hook up with these controllers if you have this program and a microphone.

and logging in. Squawk standby while you finish configuring your flight. Load up your FSNavigator flight plan, fine-tune the details in the dialog box as shown in Figure 9.10, and you'll be ready to submit your flight plan to the VATSIM network.

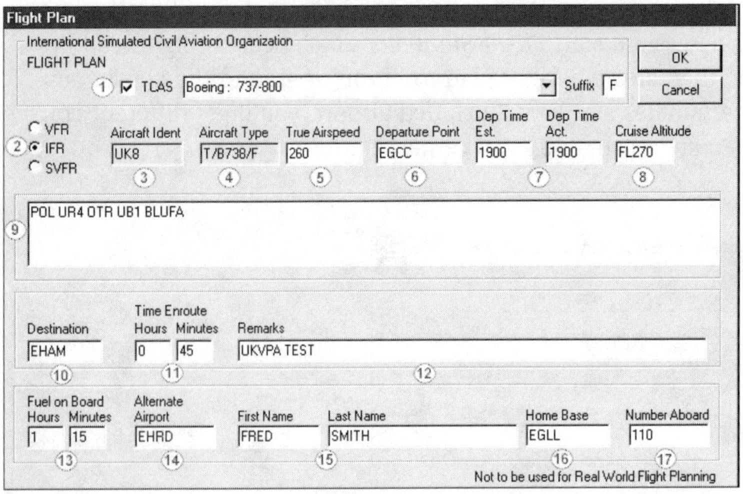

Figure 9.10 Finalizing a flight plan for submission to the VATSIM network

After you've set up your flight plan, tune your radio to the appropriate controller using the SquawkBox menu. When you're ready to go, deselect squawk standby and request departure clearance (if you're at a controlled airport). If you're bound for one, get airborne and contact the center for clearance.

Flying on the VATSIM network is as close as you can get to real-life aviation. The controllers are all very helpful, and even if you don't get the lingo just right, they won't be angry with you. They are eager to help new pilots, and as long as you can keep your own plane under control, you really have no cause for embarrassment. Listen to their instructions, feel free to ask for explanations, and admit when you don't know what they mean.

If you need to brush up on air traffic control procedures, just hop on a voice channel and listen in for a while—you'll be surprised at just how much you can learn by example. The same ATC procedures used by the computer controllers in solo play are used on VATSIM, so refer to the ATC online manual that comes with *Flight Simulator 2002* for a comprehensive primer in operations.